DATE DU

			PRINTED IN U.S.A.

RECIPES

from a

CHÂTEAU IN CHAMPAGNE

RECIPES
from a
CHÂTEAU
IN CHAMPAGNE

by

Robin McDouall and Sheila Bush

Illustrated by
Graham Rust and Philippe Jullian

LONDON
VICTOR GOLLANCZ LTD
1983

First published October 1982
Second impression January 1983

British Library Cataloguing in Publication Data
McDouall, Robin
  Recipes from a château in Champagne
  1. Cookery, French
  I. Title   II Bush, Sheila
  641.5944   TX719
  ISBN 0-575-03177-8

Made and printed in Great Britain at
The Camelot Press Ltd, Southampton

CONTENTS

COLOUR PLATES

Le Salon Rouge de Saron

INTRODUCTION

In the year when this cookery book is being published, the château de Saran celebrates its Silver Jubilee as the beautiful house, at once elegant and friendly, where the world-famous champagne firm of Moët & Chandon entertain their guests.

Those who have been fortunate enough to be invited to the château will know that it is about ninety miles east of Paris, standing above the village of Chouilly, which is three miles or so from Epernay in the heart of the Champagne district. Originally it was a *vendangeoir*, or press-house, but towards the end of the eighteenth century it was acquired by the Moët family, and for many years they used it as a hunting-lodge. Although since Roman times vineyards have stretched to the north and east of the gentle hill on which the château stands, extensive forests lie to the south and west; right up to the second world war they provided shelter for wild boar.

In about 1920 Saran was enlarged so that it could be used as a summer residence for the family. But in the mid-fifties Comte Robert-Jean de Vogüé, then the chairman of Moët & Chandon, began to feel that the firm needed somewhere where they could extend hospitality to the ever-growing number of agents, wine-merchants, hoteliers, restaurateurs, writers, journalists and other *amis de la Maison* who, with air travel becoming commonplace, were now able to visit Epernay. Saran seemed the ideal place, so in 1957 Moët took it over and modernised it to make it the wonderfully comfortable country-house it is today.

Instead of installing, as might have been expected, a French lady to be *châtelaine*, or *maîtresse de maison*, as she is also called, Monsieur de Vogüé very wisely looked across the sea to Scotland and picked Moyra Campbell, Lord Stratheden's daughter. She was the perfect choice, and for thirteen years she 'ran' the château, greeting the never-ending stream of guests of every conceivable nationality and background who come to Saran to stay or for a meal with a welcome that made them feel instantly at home. It is largely owing to her talents, and to the support which she was given by Monsieur de Vogüé, that Saran became and remains the unique place it is today.

To help her, and the *châtelaines* who succeeded her, pretty *jeunes filles* come each year, mainly from England, hovering around like so many iridescent butterflies. The word butterfly is apt, since they spread their wings only between April and October: for the rest of the year the winds blow from Siberia and the château is shut.

With great unselfishness Monsieur and Madame de Vogüé parted with their marvellous 'couple', Louis and Renée Beurton, so that they could come to Saran, Louis to be the butler and Renée the cook – and seldom was there such an inspired and creative cook. She never had any lessons. Her grandmother had been a cook but had died before Renée was born; she must have transmitted some of her gifts and secrets through her daughter, Renée's mother, whom Renée assiduously watched as a child. Many of the dishes which she served at Saran were from the old family cookery books of the de Vogüés, and it was Renée – so attractive, so helpful, so full of good sense – who established the tradition that the food should be, not *haute cuisine française*, nor even *haute cuisine bourgeoise*, but high-class French country-house cookery. This tradition has been jealousy guarded ever since by the chefs and the *châtelaines*.

Louis and Renée departed to open their own restaurant in Provence, and their place was taken by Auguste Gruas and his wife as butler and housekeeper, and by Patrice Lelaurain, a brilliant young chef who was born in nearby Rheims in 1944. His father is a well-known restaurateur – he owns La Crémaillère at Avesnes-sur-Helpe, near Laon – and this is where Patrice served his apprenticeship. After working in several distinguished restaurants he came to the Hôtel Royal Champagne (of which more presently), but was soon enticed, seconded, ordered – not for us to say which – to be chef at Saran. Of recent years he has had a talented young assistant, Patrice Auriole, to help him.

The hospitality of Moët & Chandon is such that the château de Saran, in spite of the large numbers of people who are invited there, is not big enough. So they are also entertained in Epernay itself. Many of the guests are welcomed at the Maison, as it is called – the impressive building in the Avenue de Champagne over the vast cellars where the wine is made and stored. Here there are two small reception rooms where visitors are given a glass or two of champagne: the Salon Vert, where Napoleon lunched in 1807, and the even more elegant Salon Gris next door. Both overlook what is called 'the English garden', a charming oasis of greenery.

Across the road from the Maison is the Trianon, which in 1804 was commissioned by Jean-Remy Moët, the grandson of the founder of the House, and designed by Jean-Baptiste Isabey, better known as a fashionable portrait painter and miniaturist: 'Two identical sugar-white buildings and a sunken formal French garden of quite exceptional beauty,' writes Patrick Forbes in his indispensable book *Champagne: The Wine, the Land and the People.** Beyond them is a lovely orangery.

* Victor Gollancz, 1967.

Le Jardin Anglais à la Maison Moët

One of Jean-Remy's first guests at the Trianon was the Empress Josephine. Later he entertained there practically every crowned head and man of consequence of the Europe of his day: Alexander, Tsar of Russia, Grand Duke Nicholas (the future Tsar), Grand Duke Michael, the Emperor of Austria, the Kings of Bavaria, Prussia and Saxony, the Princes of Württemberg and Baden, and Princes Schwarzenberg, Metternich, Souvaroff and Linar, not to mention Marshal Blücher and the Duke of

9

Salle à manger du Trianon

Wellington – many of them on their way to the Congress of Vienna. A later visitor was Wagner, who was a friend of the family as well as a customer.

Jean-Remy's daughter married Comte Pierre-Gabriel Chandon de Briailles, who came into the firm, bringing the name of Chandon to join Moët and so forming the household words they are today.

In 1967 Comte Jean-Louis de Maigret, a talented member of the Chandon family who had been responsible for doing up Saran, was given the task of restoring the Trianon to its pre-war splendour. It now looks very much as it must have done when Wagner was there. For many years the *maîtresse de maison* was Jean-Louis' aunt, Comtesse Emmanuel de Maigret, the Italian daughter-in-law of yet another member of the Chandon family: she combines French chic with Italian charm, and exudes a warmth and a friendliness that are irresistible.

The kitchen at the Trianon owes its excellence to the creative flair of Monsieur Joseph Thuet. Born at La Fère in Aisne, he had his first instruction in the kitchen with his uncle at the Aubergade restaurant at Pontchartrain. After attending cookery schools in Chauny and Paris he worked at the Plaza Athénée before coming to Epernay to open the reconstituted Trianon for Comte Frédéric Chandon de Briailles, then the head of Moët & Chandon. In 1972 he passed third in the whole of France in the Brevet Professionel de Cuisinier, in 1974 he became a Maître Cuisinier de France, and in 1975 a Member of the Académie Culinaire de France. He looks every inch a chef.

The third source of the recipes in this book is the Hôtel Royal Champagne at Champillon, about 3 miles out of Epernay on the road to Rheims.* In a perfect position on the hillside looking down over vineyards to the Valley of the Marne, with delightful woodland walks behind, it serves superb food, as a star and three forks in the *Guide Michelin* and membership of the Chaine de Relais et Châteaux signify. Formerly the hotel belonged to Mercier, but when Moët and Mercier amalgamated it became part of the group; today the manager is Monsieur Marcel Dellinger, and Monsieur Jean-Claude Pacherie is the head chef. For a long time the presiding genius was Monsieur André Desvignes, for over thirty years the proprietor of the Relais de Belle Aurore in Paris. The hotel

* Perhaps one day a book like ours will be written about a fourth Moët kitchen: that of the restaurant at Domaine Chandon near Yountville in the Napa Valley, where Philippe Jeanty caters for visitors to the winery which Moët established there ten years ago to produce high-quality California sparkling wines. Neither of us has visited it, but we keep on hearing that the cuisine is excellent and that one must book a table well in advance.

caters principally for its own customers, who may be staying the night, taking a meal while passing by or making a special journey to enjoy its treats; but it is also used by Moët when Saran and the Trianon are full of visitors and in the winter when Saran is shut.

So much for the setting.

le Royal Champagne

Our aim in this book is twofold. We hope to give the many thousands of people who have experienced – or will experience – Moët's hospitality a *bon souvenir* of their visit through recalling some of the excellent dishes which are served there. And we have tried to present the recipes in a form that a reasonably skilled and enthusiastic amateur cook working at home under very different conditions will not find it too difficult to reproduce. There are, of course, pitfalls: for one thing, to adapt the professionalism which a great chef brings to bear on the preparation of a dish to the much more limited possibilities of an ordinary domestic kitchen is not easy. Apart from this, there is the problem of trying to turn an art into a science – that is to say, of putting down on paper exact measurements and methods for making dishes which vary slightly every time, and which certainly evolve over the years. The chefs hardly ever measure or weigh anything, and it would be unreasonable to expect them to do so. Nor can they be expected to set down every detail of all the *plats* which they make, for in many cases this would involve page after page of instructions.

To try to overcome these problems, we asked to be allowed to spend as much time as possible in the various kitchens: to do so was an experience for which we shall always be grateful, as we are for the friendliness that invariably greeted us as we stood observing, tasting and making notes in a corner of the busy yet always orderly scene.

Though the three kitchens are very different, not only because of their different functions but because each reflects the personality of its chef, they share one feature – their extreme orderliness. Everything is shining and spick and span, with gleaming steel surfaces, glistening copper pans hanging from the ceiling, an amazing array of knives lined up for instant use, little boxes of salt, peppercorns, freshly ground pepper and chopped herbs at hand, great stoves ready for quick sautéing or gentle simmering, or to provide sufficient heat to keep a *bain-marie* going. Everyone works fast but there is never any flurry or panic, even when the *sauce béarnaise* curdles or the pastry develops cracks and has to have a discreet patch, which sometimes refreshingly happens even in the hands of these *grands maîtres*.

By around nine o'clock each morning everyone is at work. Perhaps Monsieur Thuet will have set off much earlier to the fish market in Paris, or he may be on a two-day expedition to Périgord to buy the year's supply of truffles. Work starts on all the preparatory operations involved in the cooking of the meal, the *mise en place*. At 11.30 the staff adjourn to eat their own lunch, leaving the kitchen silent, spotless and deserted. An hour later they are back again to perform the final operation.

In the brilliantly ornate salon the guests are drinking an apéritif of champagne; luncheon is announced and the company moves into the elegant dining-room – for people can wait on food but good food will not happily wait on people. Chairs are drawn back, and the food and drink are served in a formal but always friendly way.

13

Over the years Saran and the Trianon have of course changed to some extent. The guests become steadily more cosmopolitan, and with almost every race, nationality and creed to satisfy the chefs need to choose the dishes with even greater care, so that everyone can enjoy them. The menus have changed too, under the influence of modern taste and the *nouvelle cuisine*: the meals are lighter, there are fewer heavy stocks and sauces, and to a larger extent the superb quality of the food is left to speak for itself. The kitchen staffs have been cut down – at Saran there are, in fact, only three people in the kitchen, with four at the Trianon – and many processes are performed by machine rather than by hand, to the benefit of everyone.

Nevertheless, the spirit has remained unchanged. The tradition has always been that the guests are received and treated as friends, and this has continued for a quarter of a century, in the course of which thousands upon thousands of people have enjoyed an uncountable number of magnificent repasts. As one of the *châtelaines* remarked, 'Many of our guests could go to a five-star restaurant every day of their lives if they wanted to, but they wouldn't be able to enjoy what is in effect the experience of being invited to a "good class home", with cooking to match and the atmosphere of a private house.' The hospitality which Moët provides at Epernay is, in fact, unique in Champagne; and the exquisite dishes we have eaten there, the recipes for many of which we give here, reflect this far-sighted and generous philosophy.

This book could not have been attempted without the help of many people: the chefs; the former *châtelaines* (the Hon. Moyra Campbell, Comtesse Lecointre, Lady Duke, Comtesse Ponzone) and the present one, Madame Louise Danvers; Monsieur Jean-Marie Dubois, Directeur des Relations Extérieures and the *éminence grise* of Saran and the Trianon, himself a talented amateur chef; Patrick Forbes, now head of Moët & Chandon (London) Ltd, whose enthusiasm, guidance and willingness to take infinite trouble were a never-failing source of inspiration; Lady Waterpark, Miss Nancy Jarratt, Miss Anne Price and Monsieur Jean-Paul Médard. From them, and from all their colleagues with whom we have come into contact, we have had help and consideration beyond all conventional words of thanks. We should also like to express our gratitude to Mr H. I. Hutton, Harrods' meat buyer, for his very kind readiness to answer our questions.

Robin McDouall
Sheila Bush

The Dining Room at the Trianon

NOTE FOR NORTH AMERICAN READERS

Vast as North America is and great as are our resources, we do not have all of the lovely things that grow and thrive in the much smaller country of France. But it would be a great deprivation, indeed, if the lack of a few ingredients were to deter North American cooks from enjoying every one of these superb recipes. Where fresh truffles are called for, we will simply have to do without. As one who has willingly over-imbibed on several occasions at Saran and the Trianon, I can freely say that what is important is that the secrets of these creative dishes are now out of the respective kitchens and in the public domain.

And it would be foolish of me, based in New York, to list all the equivalents of a particular food. Our coasts are thousands of miles apart, our lands as varied as they are distant. One fish, the French *lotte*, has an exact equivalent here. In the North Atlantic coast waters off Canada and the United States, it is known variously as anglerfish, monkfish, bellyfish, goosefish, lawyerfish and bellowsfish! And there are other such examples. So, not wishing to complicate, I have suggested on page 59 various substitutes which can be used where necessary. In any case, most of the sauces in the fish recipes are so appealing and tasty in themselves that almost any fish would be enhanced by them.

Some cooks will not have made their own *crème fraîche* before. A good, simple direction appears in the introductory section, and I urge anyone who has not made it before to do so. First for flavour, because it approximates almost exactly the flavour – and texture – of French *crème fraîche*, a nutty, naturally matured cream, and secondly because home-made *crème fraîche* can be boiled without curdling, which commercial sour cream cannot, and because it stores well for ten days or more in the refrigerator.

Finally, *marc de champagne*. Perhaps because the making of wine on this continent does not have the ancient history of that in France, we are less familiar with some of the by-products one finds in French winefields, such as the excellent *marc de champagne*, drunk after a rich meal as a *digestif*. Our loss! If it is not to be found, the only substitute that approaches its very distinctive flavour would be Calvados, the heady apple brandy distilled from cider in Normandy.

Roberta Schneiderman
New York City, 1982

DEFINITIONS, CONVERSIONS
AND OTHER EXPLANATORY MATTERS

As readers will see, in each recipe the ingredients are set out in two columns. The left-hand column gives the Imperial and metric weights and measures, the right-hand column (which is printed in italics) the North American equivalents. These equivalents are also given in brackets and italics in the method.

Conversions

The standard conversion for dry measures from British to metric is 25 g–1 oz, which works well for most smallish quantities. However, if it is used consistently throughout the scale the final quantities will be smaller, hence the adjustment upwards after 5 oz. The conversion has, in fact, to depend on the type of recipe: if all the quantities are small, stick to the lower equivalent. The important thing is to maintain the *proportion* between the various ingredients. This applies to liquid measures also. It is above all a matter of common sense, instinct and experience, just as it is with the chefs whose recipes compose this book, and who rarely measure anything at all.

Cups and spoons are always *level*. The North American tablespoon is slightly smaller than the British one: the former weighs ¾ fl oz, the latter 1 fl oz.

Ingredients

Though some of the recipes call for rather expensive ingredients, others are within the reach of most enthusiastic cooks – and, in any case, who begrudges pushing the boat out for special occasions? The skilful cook, too, will be able to find excellent substitutes in many of the dishes – the fish, for instance. Nor is it essential to use champagne every time it is specified. At Saran, the Trianon and the Royal Champagne, of course, it is used exclusively, and there is no doubt that it imparts a special flavour which nothing else does; but a dry white wine can generally be substituted.

The same applies when the still wines of the Champagne district (known as *Coteaux Champenois*) are specified in the recipes. The chefs invariably use either the luscious *Saran*, produced by Moët & Chandon from the Chardonnay vines surrounding the château, or the delicious *Ruinart Chardonnay*, produced by Ruinart Père & Fils of Rheims, the oldest of all the champagne firms and since 1961 a member of the Moët group of companies; but any good dry white wine is a perfectly acceptable substitute.

Bouzy, which is used in three of the recipes, is a still red wine made from Pinot Noir grapes grown on the southern slopes of the Mountain of Rheims on the opposite bank of the Marne Valley facing the château de Saran. It is, however, exported in very small quantities, and here again a good red wine can be substituted.

Marc de champagne is made by distilling the liquid extract from the residue of skins and pips of grapes that have been pressed for champagne, and is aged in casks before bottling. It is accused by some of being 'fiery enough to make a goat dance', but others consider de luxe *marcs* to be the ideal *digestif*.

Flour is always plain unless specified otherwise.

Wherever possible the French names of the recipes have been translated into English. But sometimes it was impossible to find a translation which would be helpful, and in these cases we have given only the French name.

Fond Brun de Veau
(Veal Stock)

Makes 4–5 pt (2½–3 litres, 9–12 *cups*), but reduce for a more concentrated stock

2 lb (1 kg) breast of veal	*2 lb breast of veal*
1–2 calves' feet	*1–2 calves' feet*
1 lb (450 g) veal bones	*1 lb veal bones*
olive oil	*olive oil*
1 lb (450 g) onions	*1 lb onions*
8 oz (225 g) carrots	*½ lb carrots*
handful of fresh thyme and parsley	*handful of fresh thyme and parsley*
3 cloves garlic	*3 cloves garlic*
3 tbs concentrated tomato purée	*3 tbs concentrated tomato paste*
1¾ pt (1 l) red wine	*4 cups red wine*
8 pt (5 l) water	*18 cups water*
salt, pepper	*salt, pepper*

Put the veal, the calves' feet and the bones in a roasting pan and cook in a hot oven until browned.

Pour a little oil into a casserole and in this colour the chopped onions and carrots, the thyme and parsley, the unpeeled garlic cloves and the tomato purée (*paste*). When the mixture is well browned, add the veal, the calves' feet, the bones and the wine. Reduce the liquid by about half. Add the water and season lightly. Bring to a simmer and cook gently, uncovered, for 6 hours, stirring occasionally. Skim and strain. Use for sauces and gravies.

This stock can be frozen, and a supply of it in the freezer can often be extremely useful.

Fumet de Poisson
(Fish Stock)

Makes about 1½ pt
(¾ l, 3½ cups)

Fish stock is used in many of the fish recipes, and it helps to impart a delicious flavour to any fish dish. Make certain when you buy fish that your fishmonger gives you the bones and heads, which are the basis of the stock. You can make the *fumet* as you need it or – better still – make it in larger quantities and freeze it ready for use.

12 oz (350 g) fish bones and heads	*¾ lb fish bones and heads*
1 onion	*1 onion*
1 oz (25 g) butter	*2 tbs (¼ stick) butter*
sprig of thyme	*sprig of thyme*
1 bayleaf	*1 bayleaf*
a few parsley stalks	*a few parsley stalks*
1 pt (½ l) non-vintage champagne or dry white wine	*2½ cups non-vintage champagne or dry white wine*
1 pt (½ l) water or white stock	*2½ cups water or white stock*

Chop the onion and sweat it for a few minutes in the butter with the thyme, bayleaf and parsley stalks. Add the fish bones and heads and pour over the champagne or wine and the water or stock. Simmer very gently, uncovered, for 15 minutes. Strain.

Do not add any salt, for the fish stock will be reduced during the cooking of most of the recipes in which it will be used, accentuating the saltiness.

Sauce Champagne Poisson
(Champagne Fish Sauce)

This is a marvellous sauce to accompany the fish. The *fumet* must, of course, be made with champagne.

1¾ pt (1 l) fish *fumet* (see above)	*4 cups fish fumet (see above)*
½ pt (300 ml) double or whipping cream or *crème fraîche*	*1¼ cups heavy cream or crème fraîche*
7 oz (200 g) butter	*1 scant cup (1¾ sticks) butter*

Reduce the *fumet* until it is syrupy and has a glazed appearance. Add the cream and reduce again by half. Whisk in the butter, cut into small pieces, and continue to beat until the sauce is smooth and creamy.

Aspic

The Moët chefs normally make their own aspic, but sometimes they will use a commercial variety. To enrich aspic, make it partly with sherry or white wine instead of with water alone. For some recipes as much as half-and-half can be used, but the proportion of sherry or white wine to water will vary according to how delicate the aspic needs to be.

Barding

Lard 'leaves', or *bardes*, are sometimes wrapped round dry meat, poultry or game, or used to line terrines or *pâtés*, so as to give moisture and richness during the cooking. They are taken from the fat back of pork (*lard dur*), and should be cut very thin. This takes quite a lot of practice, and if your butcher can be persuaded to slice the fat for you, so much the better. Fat bacon can also generally be used for barding.

Beurre Manié

Equal quantities of flour and softened butter worked together and used to thicken sauces.

Clarified Butter

Most cooking in butter is better if clarified butter is used, since it is not so liable to burn and discolour. To clarify, put the butter in a saucepan over gentle heat, and when it has melted skim off the foam, strain into a basin and allow to set. The milky residue in the butter – which is what gives it a tendency to burn – will sink to the bottom. Once the butter has set it can be turned out, leaving the residue behind, or scooped out as needed. It is worth clarifying a good quantity at a time, keeping it ready to hand in the fridge.

Crème Anglaise
(Custard Cream)

This cream is used with many desserts. It also forms the basis of vanilla ice-cream and, with the addition of gelatine, of cold sweets such as *bavarois*, *charlottes*, etc. It has a very delicate taste.

1 pt ($\frac{1}{2}$ l) milk	*2$\frac{1}{2}$ cups milk*
vanilla pod	*vanilla bean*
5 egg-yolks	*5 egg-yolks*
5 oz (125 g) sugar	*$\frac{3}{4}$ cup sugar*

22

Bring the milk, into which you have put the vanilla pod (*bean*), slowly to the boil. Beat the egg-yolks and the sugar until they are thick and creamy and gradually pour on the milk, stirring as you do so. Return to the pan and cook gently, stirring with a wooden spoon, until the custard has thickened slightly and coats the spoon. Do not allow it to boil.

Crème Chantilly

Lightly beaten, slightly sweetened cream which is used for desserts. The cream should be chilled, and should be beaten until it is light and fluffy, but not a second longer. At the last moment a little sugar should be incorporated. The normal proportion is 1 oz (25 g, *1 heaped tablespoon*) caster (*superfine*) sugar to ½ pt (300 ml, *1¼ cups*) cream.

Crème Fleurette

This is natural untreated double cream, which is normally used by the Moët chefs for sweet dishes.

Crème Fraîche

This is used a great deal in the Moët kitchens – where there are buckets and buckets of it – as indeed it is throughout the rest of France. It is made from fresh cream which has been heated with buttermilk and left to mature, giving it a slightly sour flavour. Outside France it is not always easy to buy, but it is quite simple to make.

Stir 1 scant tablespoon of buttermilk into ½ pt (300 ml, *1¼ cups*) whipping cream and heat gently until a temperature of 85°F (30°C) is reached. Cover and leave in a warm place to thicken – the temperature should be between 60°F and 85°F (15°C and 30°C). In summer it can be kept at room temperature. The thickening process will take anything from 12–48 hours, depending on the temperature.

Once the cream has thickened it can be kept in the refrigerator for a considerable time, up to 10 days certainly, but in our experience you can keep it for far longer than this, ready to hand for those odd spoonfuls one is always needing.

The beauty of *crème fraîche* is that the faintly sour taste imparts a delicious flavour to savoury dishes, though it is also excellent with fruit and other desserts. It can be whipped, and can be boiled without curdling.

Cuire à la Nappe

An expression impossible to translate with the vividness of the original, but meaning to cook a custard or sauce until the mixture coats the spoon – an indication that it has thickened sufficiently. Use a wooden spoon, and test by passing your finger across the back of it; the mixture should not run back for a few seconds.

Déglacer (To deglaze)

To pour liquid – usually wine, but stock and cream can also be used – into a pan in which meat has been roasted, braised or fried. This dilutes the concentrated juices which have been exuded during the cooking process and turns them into a sauce.

Poaching Eggs

Bring a generous (measured) amount of water to the boil and add a quarter the quantity of white wine vinegar. Allow to boil vigorously for about 2 minutes, when the liquid will begin to break into bubbles. Carefully break each egg into one of the bubbles. Treated in this way, it is easier to prevent them from trailing strings of white.

For 6–8 eggs you will need 4 pt (2.3 l, *9 cups*) water and 1 pt ($\frac{1}{2}$ l, *$2\frac{1}{2}$ cups*) wine vinegar.

Fish Fillets

To stop the fillets from curling up during the cooking, score them lightly two or three times on the skin side, and gently beat them on both sides.

Herbs

French dishes rely so much for their delicious taste on herbs. Easy enough in summer, for even if you don't have a garden they can generally be grown in window-boxes or pots for which a space can be found somewhere. Luckily, for winter use they freeze well: mint, parsley, marjoram, basil and thyme can all be treated in this way, while tarragon can be preserved in vinegar – and this is how they do it at the Trianon.

Larding

This is the technique whereby long strips of pork fat back are inserted in beef and in game such as venison to enhance their tenderness and to carry the flavour through to the centre of the meat. It is much less used nowadays than it used to be, as we tend to avoid excess fat. There is no doubt that larding imparts an extra deliciousness to a dish such as *Boeuf Braisé à la Mode de Chez Nous* (p88), but it is quite tricky to perform the operation oneself, and rare to find a butcher who will do it for one.

A large grooved larding needle is necessary. From a piece of pork fat back, strips (lardons) should be cut about ½" (1 cm) wide. Place them in iced water to keep them firm. Following the grain of the meat, push the needle through the joint to make an opening. Take the needle out, thread the lardon though it and insert again into the hole, twisting the needle as you do so. Hold the meat firmly as you withdraw the needle, so that the lardon doesn't come out with it. Repeat at 1½"–2" (3–4 cm) intervals until all the meat has been treated in this way.

Roast Meat, Poultry and Game

Roasts should always be allowed to stand at room temperature for about 15 minutes after being taken from the oven. The meat will then be easier to carve, and, since the juices are thereby given the chance to seep back into the meat, there is less risk that it will be undercooked inside and overcooked outside.

Mushrooms

When mushrooms are being cooked in butter, always put them in the pan at the same time as the butter. In this way they keep soft, and do not become hard or over-coloured, as they may do if they are not added to the pan until the butter has melted and is hot.

Pâte à Brioche
(Brioche Dough)

This should be made several hours before you need to use it, or the day before if this is more convenient.

1½ lb (675 g) flour	*1½ lb flour*
½ oz (15 g) fresh yeast	*½ oz fresh yeast*
1 oz (25 g) sugar	*1 heaping tbs sugar*
1 tbs salt	*1 tbs salt*
6 eggs	*6 eggs*
14 oz (400 g) butter	*scant 2 cups (3½ sticks) butter*

Sieve a quarter of the flour into a small mixing-bowl and make a well in the centre. Sprinkle the yeast and a pinch of salt into 4 tbs lukewarm water and after a few minutes stir thoroughly. Pour this mixture into the well and mix to form a soft ball of dough. Make a cross on the top with a sharp knife, and place in a bowl filled with warm water just to cover. Keep the water warm but not hot in a *bain-marie*. In about 15 minutes the dough will swell to double or three times its original volume.

Put the remaining flour on a pastry board and make a well in the centre. In this put the sugar, the salt and the eggs and mix to a loose dough. When it is well mixed place on a lightly floured board and knead until the dough becomes smooth and elastic and doesn't stick to your fingers. Cream the butter until it is soft and work it into the dough.

Drain the ball of yeast dough and fold it lightly into the dough. Place in a greased bowl, cover with a warm cloth and leave to rise at room temperature, away from draughts, until it has doubled its size. Beat down, put in a plastic bag or a covered container and leave in a cold place until you are ready to use it.

Roast Pork

Unlike their English counterparts, when French cooks roast pork they do not normally keep the fat to produce crackling. It is removed and, sold under the name of *couenne*, is used, amongst other things, for lining the casseroles in which *daubes* are cooked.

Praline

4 oz (100 g) almonds	*1 cup almonds*
4 oz (100 g) sugar	*generous ½ cup sugar*

Blanch and skin the almonds and lightly brown them in the oven. Melt the sugar in a small pan with 2 tbs water, and when it is just golden (after 3 or 4 minutes) add the almonds. Stir over a moderate heat for a minute or two, then turn out on to an oiled surface and allow to cool. Pulverise in a blender or with a rolling pin and keep in an airtight container until needed.

The praline can also be made with almonds and hazelnuts mixed or with hazelnuts alone. In this case, do not skin the hazelnuts, as the brown skin adds both to the flavour and to the appearance.

Reduction

This is the boiling down process whereby the cooking liquid is reduced without the addition of any thickening element, to provide a gravy or sauce of the right consistency and taste. The art is much neglected in many kitchens outside France, but it is an important factor in obtaining the best possible results, for only in this way can you get the optimum flavour combined with the right degree of thickness or thinness. Many of the recipes in this book call for reduction, and in some cases this may seem sacrilege, if one is told to reduce half a bottle of champagne by half, then to add cream, and then to reduce by half again. But it is worth it. The results are marvellous.

It is impossible to give hard and fast rules for reducing, for it is a skill which one learns by trial and error. The nearest we can get to concrete help is to say that in general the liquid should be reduced until it resembles syrup. But this is only a guideline: an eye for the amount of reduction required will come with practice.

Truffles

These are fungi which grow underground, the most prized being the black truffles grown in the former provinces of Périgord and Quercy. They are harvested between the end of November and mid-March, but are at their best in January. They grow beneath certain species of oaks known as *truffiers* (very rarely under hornbeams and hazels), with which they have a symbiotic relationship: no other vegetation will grow there, and for this reason the ground where they are found is described as 'burnt'.

Until recently pigs (or large sows, rather) were used to sniff out the truffles. But they have a greedy habit of eating the truffles they rootle out, which involves a battle for possession of the prized objects. Nowadays, therefore, truffle hounds, which are much more amenable, are increasingly being used for the purpose.

Unhappily, the varieties of oak under which the truffles grow are not being replaced in anything like sufficient quantities. For this reason truffles are becoming scarcer and correspondingly more expensive: whereas at the beginning of the century it was not uncommon for 2,000 tonnes to be harvested, now the figure will be 100 tonnes in a good year and as low as 20–25 tonnes in a bad one. As for the price, that has now shot up to somewhere in the region of 1,400 francs per kilogram – and each kilogram will contain about 25% of earth and stones.

Vanilla Sugar

Vanilla sugar can be bought in some shops, or it can be made at home by storing a vanilla pod (*bean*) in a jar of sugar. The jar must have a tightly fitting lid.

In some of the recipes for desserts a vanilla pod is heated in milk. After use it can be rinsed, dried and returned to the jar.

Hautvillers - berceau du champagne

First Courses

Croustillon Rémois	
Croquettes de Fromage	(Cheese Croquettes)
Soufflés Helvetia	(Gruyère Cheese Soufflés)
Oeufs Brouillés Basquaise	(Scrambled Eggs with Crabmeat)
Oeufs Mont Blanc	
Terrine de Faisan	(Pheasant Terrine)
Huîtres au Champagne	(Oysters in Champagne)
Quiche de Saumon Fumé	(Smoked Salmon Quiche)
Mousseline de Brochet Curnonsky	(Mousseline of Pike)
Crêpes Soufflées au Roquefort	(Soufflé Pancakes with Roquefort Cheese)
Oeufs Trianon	(Poached Eggs with Smoked Salmon and Hollandaise Sauce)
Ramequins Champignons	(Mushroom Ramekins)
Délice du Prieur	
Tartelettes Royal Champagne	
Melon Glacé au Ratafia	(Iced Melon with Ratafia)

Croustillon Rémois

This ham and cheese concoction makes a delicious first course; cut into bite-sized pieces it is an excellent accompaniment to apéritifs.

8 oz (225 g) lean ham, in 2 thick slices	½ lb ham in 2 thick slices
8 oz (225 g) gruyère cheese	½ lb gruyère cheese
2 oz (50 g) almonds	½ cup almonds
8 large slices of bread	8 large slices of bread
salt, pepper	salt, pepper

Béchamel sauce:	*Béchamel sauce:*
1 oz (25 g) butter	2 tbs (¼ stick) butter
1 oz (25 g) flour	2 tbs flour
¼ pt (150 ml) dry white wine	generous ½ cup dry white wine
¼ pt (150 ml) chicken stock	generous ½ cup chicken stock

First make the *béchamel* sauce:

Béchamel sauce: Melt the butter and stir in the flour. Cook gently for 2 or 3 minutes without colouring. Add the hot wine and stock all at once, beating with a wire whisk until the sauce is smooth. Leave over the lowest possible heat for ten minutes or so, stirring occasionally.

Cut the ham and cheese into very small dice and mix together. Blanch and skin the almonds, slice them, and grill until they are light brown. Add the almonds to the ham and cheese mixture, season with a little salt and plenty of pepper, and add just enough of the *béchamel* sauce to bind together. You will probably not need the whole amount of sauce, as the mixture must be very stiff, or it will 'run' in the oven.

Toast the bread very lightly so that it barely changes colour and remove the crusts. Spread the ham and cheese mixture evenly over the bread and put into a hot oven (450°F, 230°C, gas mark 8) for 5 minutes, until it is browned and bubbling. If you are serving with apéritifs, cut the slices of toast into bite-sized squares or triangles.

Croquettes de Fromage
(Cheese Croquettes)

3 oz (75 g) butter
3 oz (75 g) flour
1 pt (½ l) milk
3 egg-yolks
2 oz (50 g) gruyère cheese,
  grated
2 oz (50 g) parmesan cheese,
  grated
salt, pepper, nutmeg
1 beaten egg
fresh toasted breadcrumbs
deep fat for frying
parsley to garnish

scant ½ cup (¾ stick) butter
¾ cup flour
2½ cups milk
3 egg-yolks
⅔ cup grated gruyère cheese
⅔ cup grated parmesan cheese
salt, pepper, nutmeg
1 beaten egg
fresh toasted breadcrumbs
deep fat for frying
parsley to garnish

Melt the butter and stir in the flour. Cook gently for 2 or 3 minutes without colouring. Add the hot milk all at once and beat with a wire whisk until the sauce is smooth. Remove from the heat, cool a little and add the beaten egg-yolks and the grated gruyère and parmesan cheese. Season generously with salt, pepper and freshly grated nutmeg. Spread the mixture on an oiled marble slab or wooden board and leave for several hours or overnight, until cold and set.

Form into cork-sized croquettes, coat with beaten egg and breadcrumbs and deep fry until crisp and golden brown. Serve immediately, garnished with little sprigs of fried parsley (dipped for a second in the boiling fat).

Soufflés Helvetia
(Gruyère Cheese Soufflés)

Serves 5–6, according to the size of the ramekins

4 oz (100 g) butter
½ oz (15 g) flour
¼ pt (150 ml) milk
4 oz (100 g) gruyère cheese, grated
3 eggs
salt, pepper, nutmeg

generous ½ cup (1 stick) butter
1 tbs flour
generous ½ cup milk
1½ cups grated gruyère cheese
3 eggs
salt, pepper, nutmeg

Sauce:

½ pt (300 ml) double cream or crème fraîche
1 oz (25 g) butter
½ oz (12 g) flour

Sauce:

1¼ cups heavy cream or crème fraîche
2 tbs (¼ stick) butter
1 tbs flour

Butter the ramekins generously. In a small pan melt the butter and stir in the flour. Cook gently for 2 minutes without colouring. Add the hot milk all at once and beat with a wire whisk until the sauce is smooth. Season with salt, pepper and a little freshly grated nutmeg. Off the heat add three-quarters of the grated gruyère cheese, two whole eggs and one yolk, and mix well. Fold in the remaining egg-white, stiffly beaten.

Fill the ramekins with the mixture. Cook in a *bain-marie* in a moderate oven (350°F, 180°C, gas mark 4) for 25–30 minutes.

Meanwhile, make the sauce.

Sauce: Heat the cream and enrich with *beurre manié* made by working together the butter and flour. Stir over gentle heat until the sauce has thickened and is quite smooth.

When the soufflés are cooked turn them out on to a lightly buttered fireproof serving dish and pour the sauce over them. Sprinkle the rest of the grated gruyère cheese over the top and cook in a hot oven (425°F, 220°C, gas mark 7) for 10 minutes, until the soufflés are bubbling and golden brown.

Oeufs Brouillés Basquaise
(Scrambled Eggs with Crabmeat)

For each person:
1 small slice of bread
olive oil
2 oz (50 g) tomatoes
1 oz (25 g) fresh crabmeat
1 tbs white wine
2 eggs
½ oz (15 g) butter
1 tbs cream
2–3 thin strips pimento
salt, pepper

For each person:
1 small slice of bread
olive oil
2 oz tomatoes
1 oz fresh crabmeat
1 tbs white wine
2 eggs
1 tbs (⅛ stick) butter
1 tbs cream
2–3 thin strips green pepper
salt, pepper

Cut the bread into small cubes and fry in a little olive oil until crisp. Keep warm. Peel and de-pip (*seed*) the tomatoes and squeeze out the juice. Chop and toss in a little olive oil. Heat the crabmeat very gently in the wine.

Beat the eggs and season. Melt half the butter in a basin in a *bain-marie* or in a double saucepan and pour in the eggs. Cook them gently, stirring with a wooden spoon to keep them from sticking as they set. When they are almost done stir in the rest of the butter and the cream. Turn into a serving dish and spread the crabmeat, the tomatoes and the pimento (*green pepper*) on top.

Arrange the croûtons round the edge of the dish and serve at once.

Oeufs Mont Blanc

It is best not to attempt this simple but excellent dish for more than 4 people, as the cooking has to be carefully controlled.

4 slices of bread	*4 slices of bread*
4 slices of ham	*4 slices of ham*
3 eggs	*3 eggs*
3 oz (75 g) gruyère cheese, grated	*1 generous cup grated gruyère cheese*
pepper	*pepper*
oil for frying	*oil for frying*

Preheat the oven to very hot (475°F, 240°C, gas mark 9). Cut the bread and the ham into 3″ (7 cm) rounds. Mix together the egg-yolks and the grated cheese, add a little pepper and spread this mixture on the rounds of bread. Lay the pieces of ham on top. Whip the whites very stiffly and make a dome of egg-white completely to cover the ham (this is most easily done with the concave side of a soup spoon, evening it off with a fork). You may not need all the egg-white.

Have about ½″ (1 cm) of oil, hot, but not smoking, in a large frying pan – it must be large, as the oil must remain very hot thoughout the cooking. Put in the prepared rounds of bread. As they cook, and the ham and cheese heat through, spoon the very hot oil on to the whites: they must not brown, but repeated ladling of the oil will puff them up until they swell to nearly twice their original size. When this stage is reached, put the frying pan in the oven for about half a minute, leaving the door open. Transfer the *Oeufs Mont Blanc* to a hot dish and serve at once.

Terrine de Faisan
(Pheasant Terrine)

1 pheasant	*1 pheasant*
2 lb (1 kg) lean pork	*2 lb lean pork*
1 lb (450 g) veal	*1 lb veal*
12 oz (350 g) bacon rashers	*¾ lb bacon slices*
4–6 tbs cognac	*5–7 tbs cognac*
pinch of nutmeg	*pinch of nutmeg*
pinch of dried thyme	*pinch of dried thyme*
2 bayleaves	*2 bayleaves*
2 eggs	*2 eggs*
6 tbs double cream or	*7 tbs heavy cream or*
crème fraîche	*crème fraîche*
2 oz (50 g) pistachio nuts	*⅓ cup pistachio nuts*
1 oz (25 g) truffle (optional)	*1 oz truffle (optional)*
1 sprig of fresh thyme	*1 sprig of fresh thyme*
salt, pepper	*salt, pepper*

Discard the drumsticks of the pheasant, and cut the rest of the flesh into thin slices. Place the slices in a bowl containing the cognac, a pinch of salt, pepper, nutmeg and dried thyme and one bayleaf. Leave to marinade for about 6 hours.

Mince the pork and veal finely, removing any fat, mix well and season. Fry a tiny bit to test the seasoning.

Take the pieces of pheasant out of the marinade and strain the marinade into the meat *farce*, adding the eggs and cream to bind. Mix in the chopped pistachio nuts and truffle.

Line a terrine with three-quarters of the bacon, and on this place a layer of *farce*. Next put a layer of pheasant. Alternate the *farce* and the pheasant, finishing with the *farce*. Cover with the remaining bacon, and put the second bayleaf and the sprig of fresh thyme on top. Cover the terrine with a lid or aluminium foil and cook in a *bain-marie* in a moderate oven (350°F, 180°C, gas mark 4) for about 1½ hours. Test with a skewer to see when it is cooked: the needle should come out clean, not sticky.

Serve cold, with toast and butter.

Huîtres au Champagne
Serves 6

(Oysters in Champagne)

36 oysters
¼ pt (150 ml) fish stock (see p21)
¼ pt (150 ml) non-vintage champagne or Saran
3 tbs truffle juice (optional)
¼ pt (150 ml) double or whipping cream or *crème fraîche*
2 oz (50 g) butter

36 oysters
generous ½ cup fish stock (see p21)
generous ½ cup non-vintage champagne or Saran
3 tbs truffle juice (optional)
generous ½ cup heavy cream or crème fraîche
4 tbs (½ stick) butter

Open the oysters, keeping the deep half-shells. Put them in a casserole with their liquor over a low flame until the liquid whitens. Remove from the pan and keep warm. Add to the pan the fish stock, the champagne or Saran and the truffle juice, and reduce. Stir in the cream, and reduce again until you have a rich sauce the colour of ivory. Enrich with the butter cut into small pieces. Put an oyster in each shell, cover with the sauce and serve at once.

Quiche de Saumon Fumé
(Smoked Salmon Quiche)

1 lb (450 g) smoked salmon
10 oz (275 g) puff or shortcrust
pastry
3 oz (75 g) gruyère cheese,
grated
5 eggs
¼ pt (150 ml) double cream or
crème fraîche
2 oz (50 g) arrowroot
½ pt (300 ml) milk
pinch of *quatre épices* (ground
ginger, nutmeg, cinnamon,
clove)
1 oz (25 g) caviar (optional)
salt, pepper, nutmeg

1 lb smoked salmon
10 oz puff or shortcrust pastry
1 generous cup grated gruyère
cheese
5 eggs
generous ½ cup heavy cream or
crème fraîche
⅓ cup arrowroot
1¼ cups milk
pinch of quatre épices (ground
ginger, nutmeg, cinnamon,
clove)
1 oz caviar (optional)
salt, pepper, nutmeg

Oil and flour a 10" (25 cm) flan tin. Line with the puff or shortcrust pastry. Prick the bottom with a skewer and sprinkle on the grated gruyère cheese. Cut 8 small triangles of smoked salmon for decoration and reserve. Cut the rest of the salmon into thin strips (*julienne*) and arrange evenly over the cheese.

Mix the eggs and cream well together. Stir the arrowroot very thoroughly into the milk and add. Season with salt (very sparingly, for the smoked salmon is salty), pepper and freshly ground nutmeg and add the spices. Pour into the pastry case and bake in a fairly hot oven (375°F, 190°C, gas mark 5) for about 40 minutes. Cut into slices quickly, and on each slice place a triangle of the reserved smoked salmon, and on top of that a small spoonful of caviar if you are using it. Serve hot.

As an extra touch, accompany the quiche with a cream sauce (see recipe for *Ramequins Champignons*, p42), coloured with saffron and served separately.

Mousseline de Brochet Curnonsky Serves 6
(Mousseline of Pike)

12 oz (350 g) pike flesh (or turbot or whiting)
2 eggs
4 oz (100 g) butter
⅓ pt (200 ml) double or whipping cream or *crème fraîche*
salt, pepper

¾ lb pike or whiting flesh
2 eggs
generous ½ cup (1 stick) butter
1 cup heavy cream or crème fraîche
salt, pepper

Beurre Nantais:
1 shallot
¼ pt (150 ml) dry white wine
6 oz (175 g) chilled butter

Beurre Nantais:
1 shallot
generous ½ cup dry white wine
¾ cup (1½ sticks) chilled butter

Gently poach the pike, turbot or whiting flesh, drain and chop into small pieces. Cream in a food processor. If you haven't a food processor rub through a fine sieve, or put twice through the fine blade of a mincer and pound until it is smooth. Beat in the egg-whites. Leave in the refrigerator for at least an hour. Add the butter, softened, beat in the egg-yolks one by one, mixing well, and then the cream. Season.

Butter six individual moulds and fill with the mixture. Poach gently in a *bain-marie* in a medium oven (350°F, 180°C, gas mark 4) until set (about 30 minutes). Leave in the moulds for a minute or two before turning out. Serve with *Beurre Nantais*.

Beurre Nantais: In a small pan chop the shallots very finely and cook in the wine until they are completely soft, reducing to about 1 tbs. Remove from the heat and beat in two pieces of the chilled butter, beating each piece in well. Return to a low heat and whisk in the remaining butter piece by piece, making sure that the last piece has melted before you add the next one. The sauce should be thickened and ivory coloured.

As an alternative to *Beurre Nantais*, serve the *mousseline* with the sauce which accompanies *Gratin de Fruits de Mer* (p70).

Crêpes Soufflées au Roquefort
(Soufflé Pancakes with Roquefort Cheese)

Pancakes:

4 oz (100 g) flour
1 whole egg and 1 egg-yolk
1 pt (½ l) milk
2 oz (50 g) butter
salt
oil or butter for frying

Pancakes:

1 cup flour
1 whole egg and 1 egg-yolk
2½ cups milk
4 tbs (½ stick) butter
salt
oil or butter for frying

Cheese filling:

1 oz (25 g) flour
4 whole eggs and 2 egg-whites
½ pt (300 ml) milk
6 oz (150 g) Roquefort or
    Stilton cheese, crumbled
salt, pepper

Cheese filling:

¼ cup flour
4 whole eggs and 2 egg-whites
1¼ cups milk
2 generous cups crumbled
    Roquefort or Stilton cheese
salt, pepper

Pancakes: Sift the flour and a little salt into a bowl, make a well in the centre and add the whole egg and the egg-yolk. Gradually beat in the milk. Heat the butter in a small pan to a light hazelnut colour and add. (The pancake mixture can, of course, be made in a liquidiser.) Leave in a cold place for 1 hour before making 10 pancakes in a little oil or butter in a 6″ (15 cm) pan. Keep warm while you make the cheese filling.

Cheese filling: Mix together the flour, the 4 egg-yolks and the milk. Season. Stir over a low heat with a wooden spoon until the mixture thickens and coats the spoon, but do not allow it to boil. Crumble the cheese and add. Remove from the heat, whisk the 6 egg-whites very stiff and fold into the mixture.

To assemble: Spread the pancakes out on a table. Put a big spoonful of the mixture on one half of each pancake and fold the other half over. Arrange on a well-buttered ovenproof dish with a little space between the pancakes, as they swell during the cooking. Put in a very hot oven (475°F, 240°C, gas mark 9) for 7–8 minutes. Serve at once.

Oeufs Trianon
(Poached Eggs with Smoked Salmon and Hollandaise Sauce)

6 slices brioche or milk loaf about 1¼" (3 cm) thick	*6 slices brioche or soft white bread about 1¼" thick*
6 eggs	*6 eggs*
6 small slices smoked salmon (about 3 oz, 75 g)	*6 small slices smoked salmon (about 3 oz)*
1 oz caviar (optional)	*1 oz caviar (optional)*
Sauce Hollandaise:	*Sauce Hollandaise:*
6 oz (175 g) clarified butter	*1 scant cup (6 oz) clarified butter*
3 egg-yolks	*3 egg-yolks*
½ small lemon	*½ small lemon*
salt	*salt*

Start by making the *Sauce Hollandaise*:

Sauce Hollandaise: Melt the clarified butter but do not let it get hot. Put the egg-yolks in a basin with 1 tbs water. Set over a pan of hot, but not boiling, water and whisk vigorously until the mixture thickens. Remove from the heat and very gradually add the clarified butter, beating hard all the time. When the sauce is thick and creamy add the lemon juice and a little salt, cover, and put on one side of the stove to keep warm.

Trim the slices of bread into an oval shape and hollow each slice out in the middle. Toast lightly and keep warm while you poach the eggs. Arrange the pieces of toast on a warm serving-dish and put on each a slice of smoked salmon, a coffee-spoon of caviar if you are using it, and a well-drained egg. Cover with the sauce and serve at once.

Ramequins Champignons
(Mushroom Ramekins)

12 oz (350 g) mushrooms	¾ lb mushrooms
1 oz (25 g) butter	2 tbs (¼ stick) butter
½ oz (12 g) cornflour	1 tbs cornstarch
3 eggs	3 eggs
¼ pt (150 ml) double or whipping cream or crème fraîche	generous ½ cup heavy cream or crème fraîche
salt, pepper, nutmeg	salt, pepper, nutmeg

Cream Sauce:	Cream Sauce:
2 shallots	2 shallots
1 oz (25 g) butter	2 tbs (¼ stick) butter
6 tbs (100 ml) dry white wine	7 tbs dry white wine
¼ pt (150 ml) double or whipping cream or crème fraîche	generous ½ cup heavy cream or crème fraîche
salt, pepper	salt, pepper
parsley or chervil to garnish	parsley or chervil to garnish

Finely chop the mushrooms (caps and stems) and squeeze them in a cloth to extract the water. Sweat them in the butter for 5–10 minutes. Mix well together the cornflour (*cornstarch*), the eggs and the cream, making certain that the mixture is well amalgamated. Stir into the mushrooms. Season with salt, pepper and freshly grated nutmeg.

Well butter 6 ramekins. Pour the mixture into them to within ½″ (1 cm) of the top. Cook in a *bain-marie* in a low oven (250°F, 120°C, gas mark ½) for 1–1¼ hours, or until they are firm to the touch. Remove from the oven and leave in the *bain-marie* for 10 minutes.

While they are cooking, make the cream sauce:

Cream sauce: Chop the shallots finely and sweat them in the butter. When they are soft *déglacez* the pan with the white wine and reduce until there is only about 1 tablespoon left. Add the cream, season, and simmer for about 10 minutes. Strain.

Turn out the ramekins on to a warmed serving dish and pour the sauce round them. Garnish each one with a little sprig of parsley or chervil.

1 medium onion
butter ⎱
oil ⎰ for frying
4 tomatoes
2 eggs
4 oz (100 g) mushrooms
4 slices of bread
4 tbs gruyère cheese, grated
salt, pepper

1 medium onion
butter ⎱
oil ⎰ *for frying*
4 tomatoes
2 eggs
¼ lb mushrooms
4 slices of bread
4 tbs grated gruyère cheese
salt, pepper

Chop the onion finely and sweat in a little butter. When it is soft add the skinned, de-pipped (*seeded*) and roughly chopped tomatoes. Hard-boil the eggs and chop them. Slice the mushrooms finely and cook them in a little butter for about 5 minutes. Mix all together and season.

Keep warm while you fry the bread in oil and butter. Arrange on a fireproof dish, spread the mixture on top, sprinkle on the grated gruyère cheese and brown under the grill.

8 oz (225 g) puff pastry	*½ lb puff pastry*
2 eggs	*2 eggs*
8 oz (225 g) onion	*½ lb onions*
1 oz (25 g) butter	*2 tbs (¼ stick) butter*
8 oz (225 g) mushrooms	*½ lb mushrooms*
8 oz (225 g) tomatoes	*½ lb tomatoes*
4 oz (100 g) gruyère cheese, grated	*1½ cups grated gruyère cheese*
salt, pepper	*salt, pepper*

Béchamel sauce:

1 oz (25 g) butter	*2 tbs (¼ stick) butter*
1 oz (25 g) flour	*2 tbs flour*
½ pt (300 ml) milk	*1¼ cups milk*
2 tbs cream	*2 tbs cream*
salt, pepper	*salt, pepper*

Line 6 3½″ (9 cm) pastry moulds with the puff pastry. Cut 6 pieces of foil into small circles and press them down over the pastry. Bake in a hot oven (450°F, 230°C, gas mark 8) for 15 minutes. After about 10 minutes press the foil down again, if the pastry has puffed up, and return to the oven. For the last three minutes or so to remove the foil so that the bottom of the pastry will brown.

Hard-boil the eggs.

Slice the onions finely and sweat them in the butter until they are golden. Add the chopped mushrooms and continue to cook. Skin and de-pip (*seed*) the tomatoes, chop coarsely and add. Season to taste and continue to cook gently.

Meanwhile make the *béchamel* sauce.

Béchamel sauce: Melt the butter and stir in the flour. Cook gently for 2–3 minutes without colouring. Add the hot milk all at once and beat with a wire whisk until the sauce is smooth. Stir in the cream and season lightly.

Stir the *béchamel* sauce into the vegetable mixture. Check the seasoning and add the hard-boiled eggs cut in slices.

Divide this mixture between the hot pastry cases. Sprinkle with the grated gruyère cheese and brown under the grill. Serve immediately.

Melon Glacé au Ratafia
(Iced Melon with Ratafia)

The best melons to use are canteloup or cavaillon; if neither is obtainable, ogen can be used instead. Ratafia – the strong, peach-coloured aperitif of the Champagne district, made by adding cognac to the pure juice of champagne grapes – makes a delicious change from the more usual *melon au porto*. In the United States the equivalent of ratafia is Panache, produced by Domaine Chandon in California.

For each person:	*For each person:*
½ canteloup or cavaillon melon	*½ small canteloupe melon*
1 small tbs ratafia	*1 tbs Panache*

Scoop the pulp and seeds out of the melon and cut a tiny slice from the bottom so that it will stand comfortably on the plate. Pour the ratafia into the cavity and put in the refrigerator for at least 2 hours. This period of soaking softens the taste of the ratafia, and gives the melon a marvellously subtle flavour.

Les Vendanges

Soups

Crème Julienne Darblay	(Leek and Potato Soup)
Crème Dubarry	(Cauliflower Soup)
Crème de Tomates	(Tomato Soup)
Crème de Céleri-Rave	(Celeriac Soup)
Soupe de Moules	(Mussel Soup)
Consommé de Volaille avec Cresson	(Chicken Consommé with Watercress)
Pot-au-Feu ou Petite Marmite	
Velouté de Soles	(Sole Velouté Soup)

The View from Saran overlooking the Marne Valley

Crème Julienne Darblay   *Serves 8*
(Leek and Potato Soup)

8 oz (225 g) leeks, white part only

2 lb (1 kg) potatoes

2 oz (50 g) butter

2½ pt (1¼ l) water

4 oz (100 g) carrots

4 oz (100 g) celery

½ pt (300 ml) double or whipping cream or *crème fraîche*

salt, pepper, sugar

chervil or parsley for garnish

½ lb leeks, white part only

2 lb potatoes

4 tbs (½ stick) butter

6 cups water

¼ lb carrots

¼ lb celery

1¼ cups heavy cream or *crème fraîche*

salt, pepper, sugar

chervil or parsley for garnish

Chop three-quarters of the leeks and sweat them in three-quarters of the butter. Add the potatoes, peeled and cut into quarters, and the boiling water. Season, cover and cook until the vegetables are soft (about 20 minutes). Liquidise with the cooking liquor and return to the pan.

While the leeks and potatoes are cooking, cut the carrot, the celery and the reserved leek into fine *julienne* strips, and sweat them in the remaining butter with a little sugar and salt. Add to the soup and stir in the cream. Correct the seasoning and reheat.

Just before serving sprinkle in some chopped parsley or chervil.

Crème Dubarry
(Cauliflower Soup)

1 large cauliflower
6 oz (150 g) leeks, white part
   only
4 oz (100 g) butter
2 oz (50 g) flour
2½ pt (1¼ l) water
¼ pt (150 ml) double or
   whipping cream or *crème*
   fraîche
3 egg-yolks
salt, pepper
chervil or parsley for garnish

1 large cauliflower
6 oz leeks, white part only
generous ½ cup (1 stick) butter
½ cup flour
6 cups water
generous ½ cup heavy cream or
   crème fraîche
3 egg-yolks
salt, pepper
chervil or parsley for garnish

Chop the leeks and sweat them in the butter for about 10 minutes. Add the flour, stirring it in well for 5 minutes or so. Pour in the hot water and season. Bring to the boil and add the cauliflower, cut up, but leaving a few small florets on one side for garnish. Cover and simmer gently until the cauliflower is cooked (about 20 minutes). Meanwhile blanch the reserved florets until they are soft (5–10 minutes).

Liquidise the soup, return to the pan and thicken with the cream mixed with the beaten egg-yolks. Reheat, but do not allow to boil. Add the drained cauliflower florets, correct the seasoning, and serve, garnished with a sprinkling of chopped chervil or parsley.

Crème de Tomates
(Tomato Soup)

2 lb (1 kg) tomatoes	*2 lb tomatoes*
8 oz (225 g) onions	*½ lb onions*
2 oz (50 g) butter	*4 tbs (½ stick) butter*
1¾ pt (1 l) chicken stock	*4 cups chicken stock*
½ pt (300 ml) double or whipping cream or *crème fraîche*	*1¼ cups heavy cream or crème fraîche*
salt, pepper, sugar	*salt, pepper, sugar*
parsley for garnish	*parsley for garnish*

Chop the onions and sweat them in the butter until they are golden and glistening. Add the tomatoes, roughly chopped, cover the pan, and simmer until the onions are soft. Add the hot stock, season with salt, pepper and a little sugar, cover once more, and simmer for 20 minutes over a low heat. Liquidise, strain, and return to the pan.

Stir in the cream, correct the seasoning and reheat. Serve garnished with chopped parsley.

Crème de Céleri-Rave
(Celeriac Soup)

2 medium celeriac
juice of ½ lemon
½ pt (300 ml) double or
   whipping cream or *crème*
   fraîche
½ pt (300 ml) milk
2 oz (50 g) butter
salt, pepper
parsley or chives for garnish

2 medium celery root
juice of ½ lemon
1¼ cups heavy cream or crème
   fraîche
1¼ cups milk
4 tbs (½ stick) butter
salt, pepper
parsley or chives for garnish

Peel the celeriac (*celery roots*), cut them up and squeeze the lemon juice over them. Cook in just enough salted water to cover until they are soft (15–20 minutes). Liquidise with most of the cooking liquid. Return to the pan and add the cream and the hot milk. Bring to the boil, adding more of the cooking liquid, if necessary, to bring to the desired consistency. Strain, return to the pan and add the butter. Check the seasoning and serve garnished with chopped parsley or chives.

Soupe de Moules
(Mussel Soup)

3 pt (1½ l) mussels	*3 lb mussels*
2 oz (50 g) butter	*4 tbs (½ stick) butter*
2 tbs olive oil	*2 tbs olive oil*
4 oz (100 g) carrots	*¼ lb carrots*
4 oz (100 g) onions	*¼ lb onions*
4 oz (100 g) leeks	*¼ lb leeks*
2½ pt (1¼ l) fish stock (see p21)	*6 cups fish stock (see p21)*
8 oz (225 g) tomatoes	*½ lb tomatoes*
½ gill (75 ml) dry white wine	*⅓ cup dry white wine*
½ gill (75 ml) water	*⅓ cup water*
¼ pt (150 ml) double or whipping cream or *crème fraîche*	*generous ½ cup heavy cream or crème fraîche*
salt, pepper, saffron	*salt, pepper, saffron*

Melt half the butter with all the oil. Dice the carrots, chop the onions and the leeks finely and turn them in the fat, cooking them until softened. Add the stock to the pan, followed by the tomatoes, skinned, de-pipped (*seeded*) and chopped. Bring to the boil. Season with salt, pepper, and a generous pinch of saffron infused in a cupful of the hot stock. Cover the pan and simmer for 40 minutes while you prepare the mussels.

Scrub under cold running water, discarding any that are not tightly shut. Put them in a large, heavy pan with the white wine and water and set over a brisk heat for 5 minutes, shaking the pan occasionally to spread the heat, until the mussels open. Discard any that do not open. Strain, and add the cooking liquor to the soup.

When ready to serve, remove the soup from the heat and whisk in the remaining butter and the cream. Add the mussels, top shells and beards removed, just before serving.

Consommé de Volaille avec Cresson
(Chicken Consommé with Watercress)

1 small boiling fowl	*1 small boiling fowl*
bouquet garni	*bouquet garni*
2 leeks	*2 leeks*
2 tomatoes	*2 tomatoes*
1 carrot	*1 carrot*
stick of celery	*stick of celery*
4 pt (2¼ l) water	*9 cups water*
2 egg-whites	*2 egg-whites*
1 bunch watercress	*1 bunch watercress*
salt, pepper	*salt, pepper*

Remove the skin and fat from the boiling fowl and put it in a large pot. Add the bouquet garni and the chopped vegetables, reserving the green from one of the leeks. Season. Add the water, cover and simmer gently for 4 hours. Skim off the fat and strain the stock.

To clarify the stock, mix together the egg-whites, the reserved leek green, finely chopped, and a little water. Add to the stock and whisk slowly over a low heat until the whites attract any impurities to the surface. As soon as simmering point is reached, stop whisking. Leave over the lowest possible heat, barely bubbling, for 15 minutes. Skim, and strain again through a fine cloth.

Chop a generous handful of watercress very finely, bring the consommé to the boil, correct the seasoning and throw in the watercress just before serving.

Pot-au-Feu ou Petite Marmite

1 lb (450 g) beef skirt	*1 lb steak skirt*
1 lb (450 g) top rib	*1 lb top rib*
4 oz (100 g) marrow bone	*¼-lb piece marrow bone*
5 pt (3 l) water	*12 cups water*
4 oz (100 g) carrots	*¼ lb carrots*
¼ celery head	*¼ celery heart*
3 oz (75 g) turnips	*3 oz turnips*
3 oz (75 g) trimmed leeks	*3 oz trimmed leeks*
2 medium onions	*2 medium onions*
¼ medium cabbage	*¼ medium cabbage*
giblets from 2 chickens	*giblets from 2 chickens*
coarse salt	*coarse salt*
8 oz (200 g) bread	*½ lb bread*

Into a very large pan put the meat, the marrow bone tied in a piece of muslin (to retain the marrow), the water and some coarse salt. Bring to the boil slowly and skim until clear.

Meanwhile prepare the vegetables: cut the carrots, celery and turnips *julienne* and slice the leeks. Slice the onions thickly and brown under the grill. Add all these to the pan, together with the cabbage squeezed into a ball. Partially cover and simmer very gently for 4 hours. One hour before cooking is complete add the chicken giblets.

To serve, skim the fat from the bouillon – not too thoroughly – and remove the marrow bone. Scoop out the marrow and return it to the pot. Serve the bouillon with thin slices of bread, crisped in the oven.

For the ordinary household, the deliciously tender meat can be kept for another occasion.

Velouté de Soles
(Sole Velouté Soup)

1 lb (450 g) sole fillets	*1 lb sole fillets*
4 oz (100 g) mushrooms	*¼ lb mushrooms*
3 oz (75 g) butter	*scant ½ cup (¾ stick) butter*
1 tbs cornflour	*1 tbs cornstarch*
½ pt (300 ml) double or	*1¼ cups heavy cream or crème*
whipping cream or *crème*	* fraîche*
fraîche	*3 egg-yolks*
3 egg-yolks	*2½ cups fish stock (see p21)*
1 pt (½ l) fish stock (see p21)	*salt, pepper*
salt, pepper	*chervil or parsley for garnish*
chervil or parsley for garnish	

Remove the skin from the sole fillets and cut them into small pieces (*goujonettes*) about ½" (1 cm) wide and 2" (5 cm) long.

Slice the mushrooms finely and sweat them in two-thirds of the butter. Set aside.

Mix the cornflour (*cornstarch*) with a little of the cream, then add the beaten egg-yolks and the rest of the cream. Carefully stir into the hot fish stock, season, and continue to stir over a low heat until the *velouté* thickens. Do not allow it to boil. It should have the consistency of cream, so add a little more fish stock, cream or milk if it is too thick. Test for seasoning. Stir in the rest of the butter, cut into small pieces, and add the mushrooms.

In a separate pan, quickly poach the *goujonettes* in just enough water to cover them. They will be cooked in literally 1 minute. Drain well and add to the *velouté*.

Serve in soup bowls, garnished with a little chopped parsley or chervil.

le Grand Foudre

Fish Substitutes

Saumon au Champagne	(Salmon Cooked in Champagne)
Escalope de Saumon au Champagne et à l'Oseille	(Salmon Cooked in Champagne with Sorrel)
Terrine de Saumon en Gelée, Sauce Grelette	(Terrine of Salmon with Tomato Sauce)
Filets de Sole 'Délices de Lucat'	
Filets de Sole Miroton	(Sole with Mushrooms)
Julienne de Sole à l'Orange	(Sole with Orange Sauce)
Sole Catalane au Brut Impérial	(Sole with Tomatoes Cooked in Champagne)
Coquilles St Jacques à la Nage	(Scallops with Herbs)
Coquilles St Jacques Bonne Femme	
Gratin de Fruits de Mer	
Bar au Fenouil	(Sea Bass with Fennel)
Bar en Bellevue	(Sea Bass with Mayonnaise)
Gâteau de Turbotin aux Epinards	(Turbot with Spinach)
Turbot Maître d'Hôtel Braisé au Saran	(Braised Turbot with Maître d'Hôtel Butter)
Colin Provençale	(Hake Baked with Tomatoes)
Colin Concombres aux Fines Herbes	(Hake with Cucumber and *Fines Herbes)*
Rougets dans leur Nage	(Red Mullet with *Sauce Hollandaise*)
Lotte aux Ecrevisses et au Brut Impérial	(Monkfish with Crayfish in Champagne)

Fish Substitutes

One morning while one of us was staying at the Trianon, Monsieur Thuet went off very early to the Paris fish-market. He came back with about six large *paniers* filled with gleaming fish of every imaginable type: salmon, sole, *écrevisses*, prawns, mullet, monkfish, and several other varieties. It was a sight quite beautiful to behold.

Short of going to the fish-market oneself, it is no longer possible to buy many of these fish except in fishmongers of very high quality; and with the present trend it looks as if we shall find it increasingly difficult to buy any 'wet' fish at all. So one must look for substitutes.

When we discussed this problem with the Moët chefs they suggested the following possible alternatives:

Sea bass	Red or grey mullet
Turbot	Brill or halibut
Hake	Cod, haddock or any firm-fleshed white fish

For North America the following substitutes are suggested:

Hake	Cod or scrod. For hake steaks halibut can be used as an alternative
Sea bass	Striped bass
Turbot	Flounder, fluke or halibut

Saumon au Champagne
(Salmon Cooked in Champagne)

Serves 8

An extravagant but delectable dish.

1 salmon about 6½ lb (3 kg)
6 shallots
1 lb (450 g) mushrooms ✕
1 bottle non-vintage
   champagne
1 teasp lemon juice
¾ pt (425 ml) double or
   whipping cream or *crème
   fraîche*
2 oz (50 g) butter
salt, pepper

*1 salmon about 6½ lb
6 shallots
1 lb mushrooms
1 bottle non-vintage champagne
1 teasp lemon juice
1¾ cups heavy cream or crème
   fraîche
4 tbs (½ stick) butter
salt, pepper*

✕ Reserve 10 whole mushrooms

The salmon can be cooked with or without the head, according to the size of your baking-pan. Butter the pan generously and put the salmon in it, together with the finely chopped shallots and mushrooms. Keep back 10 mushroom caps for garnish. Add the champagne, season, and cook uncovered in a hot oven (450°F, 230°C, gas mark 8) for ¾ hour, basting from time to time. Meanwhile poach the 10 mushroom caps in water with a little lemon juice. ✕

Take the salmon out of the pan, drain it and skin it. Put it on a big serving dish and keep warm. Strain the cooking liquor, reserving the shallots and mushrooms, and reduce rapidly. Add the cream and reduce again. Liquidise the mushrooms and shallots and stir into the sauce, continuing to reduce, if necessary, until the sauce is thick and creamy – but probably the mushrooms will thicken it sufficiently. Finish with the butter cut into small pieces and whisked in. Pour the sauce over the salmon, drain the mushroom caps and arrange them on top.

This is a good dish for a dinner party, since the salmon can be cooked and skinned just before the guests arrive, wrapped in foil and kept in a warm place. You can then make the sauce, and either keep it warm in a *bain-marie* or reheat it when you are ready to serve the fish.

Escalope de Saumon au Champagne et à l'Oseille   Serves 4
(Salmon Cooked in Champagne with Sorrel)

4 salmon steaks each weighing about 4 oz (100 g)
1 lb (450 g) sorrel, or spinach with a little lemon juice
about 6 oz (150 g) butter
6 tbs double or whipping cream or *crème fraîche*
flour, salt, pepper

Fish stock:

8 oz (225 g) sole bones and heads
1 onion
nut of butter
small bouquet garni
½ pt (300 ml) non-vintage champagne

4 salmon steaks each weighing about ¼ lb
1 lb sorrel, or spinach flavoured with a little lemon juice
about ¾ cup (1½ sticks) butter
7 tbs heavy cream or crème fraîche
flour, salt, pepper

Fish stock:

½ lb sole bones and heads
1 onion
pat of butter
small bouquet garni
1¼ cups non-vintage champagne

First make the fish stock:

Fish stock: Chop the onion and gently sweat it in the butter. Add the fish bones and heads, the bouquet garni and the champagne. Simmer for 10 minutes uncovered. Strain and reduce by about half.

Chop the sorrel very finely and sweat it in about a third of the butter, bubbling to evaporate the excess moisture. When it is soft season, arrange on a serving dish and keep warm.

Coat the salmon steaks in seasoned flour and fry gently in half the remaining butter until they are cooked through. Arrange on top of the sorrel.

Add the cream to the fish stock and reduce again to about ¼ pt (150 ml, *generous ½ cup*). Whisk in the rest of the butter, correct the seasoning and pour over the fish.

Terrine de Saumon en Gelée, Sauce Grelette

Serves 6 as a starter,
4 as a main course

(Terrine of Salmon with Tomato Sauce)

1 lb (450 g) salmon
bare ¼ pt (125 ml) white wine
1 pt (generous ½ l) aspic, made
  with ¾ water and ¼ sherry
2 hard-boiled eggs
1½ tbs finely chopped chervil or
  parsley
1 tbs finely chopped
  tarragon
1–1½ lemons
salt, pepper

1 lb salmon
½ cup white wine
2½ cups aspic, made with ¾ water
  and ¼ sherry
2 hard-boiled eggs
2 tbs finely chopped chervil or
  parsley
1 tbs finely chopped tarragon
1–1½ lemons
salt, pepper

Sauce Grelette:

6 oz (175 g) tomatoes
1–2 tbs olive oil
⅓ pt (200 ml) double or
  whipping cream or *crème
  fraîche*
1 tbs *fines herbes*
salt, cayenne pepper

Sauce Grelette:

6 oz tomatoes
1–2 tbs olive oil
1 cup heavy cream or crème fraîche
1 tbs fines herbes
salt, cayenne pepper

Remove the skin and bone from the salmon. Cut it into strips 1″ (2 cm) wide, and cut these strips into 1″ (2 cm) cubes. Marinade in the white wine, with salt and pepper, for 1 hour. Meanwhile make the aspic with ¾ water and ¼ sherry, and put in the freezer or fridge so that it will begin to set.

Peel and chop coarsely the hard-boiled eggs. Finely chop the chervil or parsley and the tarragon. Peel the lemon, carefully removing all the pith, and cut the zest into tiny dice. Blanch for a few minutes and drain.

Gently poach the salmon in its marinade for 3 minutes. Pour off the liquid and drain the fish well on a cloth.

Pour a little of the aspic into a mould. Sprinkle on some of the lemon zest, chopped herbs and eggs. Put in the freezer. When it has set, lay on this bed some of the salmon cubes, then repeat with the eggs, herbs and lemon, and pour over more of the jelly. Refrigerate once again. Repeat until all has been used up. The aspic must completely cover the mixture.

Sauce Grelette: Peel the tomatoes, remove the pips (*seeds*) and chop the flesh coarsely. Sautez in a little oil until all the liquid has evaporated and the tomato has reduced to a purée. Remove from the heat and add the whipped cream, together with a generous tablespoon of *fines herbes* finely chopped. Season with salt and cayenne pepper and allow to cool.

When you are ready to serve, unmould the salmon and either pour the *Sauce Grelette* round it or serve separately.

Filets de Sole 'Délices de Lucat'   Serves 4

8 sole fillets	*8 sole fillets*
8 oz (225 g) mushrooms	*½ lb mushrooms*
8 oz (225 g) tomatoes	*½ lb tomatoes*
½ pt (300 ml) dry white wine	*1¼ cups dry white wine*
1 oz (25 g) butter	*2 tbs (¼ stick) butter*
1 oz (25 g) flour	*2 tbs flour*
¼ pt (150 ml) double or	*generous ½ cup heavy cream or*
whipping cream or *crème*	*crème fraîche*
fraîche	*salt, pepper*
salt, pepper	

> Beurre manie (handwritten annotation)

Make 3 shallow cuts on the skin side of each fillet and beat lightly on both sides, to prevent them from curling at the edges. Butter a fireproof dish, fold the fillets in two with the slits inside and arrange them in the dish in one layer. Chop the mushrooms and scatter them over the fish. Peel and de-pip (*seed*) the tomatoes, chop them coarsely, and spread over the mushrooms. Add the wine, season, cover the dish and cook for 15 minutes in a hot oven (400°F, 200°C, gas mark 6).

Remove the fish to a serving dish and keep warm. Strain the hot liquid into a pan, reserving the mushrooms and tomatoes. Reduce the cooking liquid by about a third. Make a *beurre manié* by working together the butter and flour, add to the liquid and stir over a moderate heat until the sauce thickens. Add the mushrooms and tomatoes and the cream and continue to stir for 2 or 3 more minutes. Pour the sauce over the fish and serve.

Filets de Sole Miroton
(Sole with Mushrooms)

8 sole fillets
8 oz (225 g) mushrooms
2 shallots
2 oz (50 g) butter
¼ pt (150 ml) double or
    whipping cream or *crème*
    fraîche
½ pt (300 ml) fish stock (see
    p21)
salt, pepper

8 sole fillets
½ lb mushrooms
2 shallots
4 tbs (½ stick) butter
generous ½ cup heavy cream or
    crème fraîche
1¼ cups fish stock (see p21)
salt, pepper

Clean and wash the mushrooms, chop them finely and squeeze out all the juice in a cloth. Slice the shallots finely and sweat them in a quarter of the butter, add the mushrooms and cook over gentle heat for a few minutes. Stir in 1 tbs cream, season, cover the pan and simmer gently for 20 minutes. Keep warm.

Put the fillets of sole in one layer in a buttered fireproof dish, pour the fish stock over them, cover, and gently poach them. When they are cooked through lift from the dish, drain well and keep warm. Reduce the cooking liquid to about half, add the cream and reduce again, stirring all the time. When the sauce has reduced sufficiently enrich it with the rest of the butter, cut in small pieces and stirred in.

Arrange half the fillets on a serving dish, put the mushroom purée on top and cover with the remainder of the fillets. Pour the sauce over them and serve.

The Kitchen at the Hôtel Royal Champagne

Julienne de Sole à l'Orange
(Sole with Orange Sauce)

8 sole fillets	*8 sole fillets*
2 lb (1 kg) spinach	*2 lb spinach*
8 oz (225 g) chilled butter	*½ lb (2 sticks) chilled butter*
2 oranges	*2 oranges*
salt, pepper	*salt, pepper*

Blanch the spinach in boiling salted water for 5 minutes, drain, and refresh in cold water. Squeeze out all the liquid, chop roughly, and put in a pan with a quarter of the butter. Cover and cook gently for 10–15 minutes. Keep warm.

Finely grate the rind of the oranges and blanch in boiling water for 3 minutes. Drain and reserve.

Cut the sole fillets into strips 3" (7 cm) by ½" (1 cm) and steam or gently poach in the minimum amount of water. Keep warm.

Dice the remaining butter. Put the juice from the oranges into a small pan, reduce until only about 1½ tbs remains, strain and return to the pan. Off the heat, beat in 2 pieces of the butter. Return the pan to a low heat and continue to add the butter, a piece at a time, vigorously whisking in each piece as you add it, until the sauce is smooth and creamy. Do not let the sauce separate or all you will have is melted butter. Season.

Arrange the spinach round the edge of a warmed serving dish, put the fish in the middle and cover with the orange sauce. Sprinkle with the reserved orange rind. Serve at once.

Sole Catalane au Brut Impérial
(Sole with Tomatoes Cooked in Champagne)

Part of the appeal of this dish lies in the striking contrast between red and white. When you buy the sole, ask your fishmonger for the bones and heads, as you will need these for the stock.

16 small sole fillets	*16 small sole fillets*
about 2½ oz (65 g) butter	*4 tbs (generous ½ stick) butter*
1½ oz (40 g) flour	*3 tbs flour*
½ pt (300 ml) double or whipping cream or *crème fraîche*	*1¼ cups heavy cream or crème fraîche*
1 onion	*1 onion*
1 tbs olive oil	*1 tbs olive oil*
8 large tomatoes	*8 medium tomatoes*
salt, pepper	*salt, pepper*

Fish stock:	*Fish stock:*
bones and heads from the fish	*bones and heads from the fish*
2 onions	*2 onions*
nut of butter	*pat of butter*
few sprigs of parsley	*few sprigs of parsley*
½ bottle non-vintage champagne	*½ bottle non-vintage champagne*
¾ pt (425 ml) white stock	*scant 2 cups white stock*
salt, pepper	*salt, pepper*

Start by making the fish stock:

Fish stock: Chop the onions and sweat them in the nut (*pat*) of butter, with the parsley, for 10–15 minutes. Add the fish bones and heads, the champagne and the stock, a little salt and a pinch of pepper. Bring to the boil and simmer, uncovered, for not more than 10 minutes. Strain and reserve.

Return the bones to the pan, add 1¾ pt (1 l, *4 cups*) water, bring to the boil and cook uncovered for 10 minutes. Strain and reserve separately this second lot of fish stock.

Make three cuts on each fillet of fish on the skin side and gently beat both sides (this will prevent the fish from curling up). Roll up each fillet from the tail, secure with a toothpick and arrange in one layer in a fireproof dish.

Next make the sauce. Melt two-thirds of the butter in a pan and stir in the flour. Cook gently for 3 or 4 minutes before adding the first lot of fish stock. Bring to the boil and continue to cook, stirring, until the sauce has reduced somewhat. Add the cream, season and reduce again until the sauce has the consistency of thickish cream. Cover, and leave in a *bain-marie*.

Chop the onion very finely and sweat gently in the olive oil until it is soft. Strain, getting rid of all the oil. Peel and halve the tomatoes, take out the pips (*seeds*) and place in a shallow ovenproof dish just large enough to hold them. Put a tiny bit of butter in each, and a coffeespoon of the onion. Cook in a very hot oven until the tomatoes are soft (about 5 minutes).

While the tomatoes are cooking bring the second lot of fish stock to the boil and pour it over the sole fillets. Cover and poach very gently for the minimum time – a few minutes will suffice. Lift them out of the dish, drain well and remove the toothpicks.

Put one fillet in each of the tomatoes, standing them endways on (*lengthwise*). Pour a spoonful of the sauce on each fillet and put the dish under a very hot grill for a few moments until the fillets are golden – but watch to see that they don't burn. Transfer to the serving dish – this must be done very carefully, or the tomatoes may break – and pour the rest of the sauce round them.

Coquilles St Jacques à la Nage
(Scallops with Herbs)

Serves 4

8–12 scallops, according to size
1 medium onion
4 oz (100 g) carrots
2 oz (50 g) butter
⅓ pt (200 ml) Ruinart Chardonnay or dry white wine
⅓ pt (200 ml) fish stock (see p21)
bouquet garni
2 tbs double or whipping cream or *crème fraîche*
salt, pepper
parsley, chives, tarragon to garnish

8–12 sea scallops, according to size
1 medium onion
¼ lb carrots
4 tbs (½ stick) butter
1 scant cup Ruinart Chardonnay or dry white wine
1 scant cup fish stock (see p21)
bouquet garni
2 tbs heavy cream or crème fraîche
salt, pepper
parsley, chives, tarragon to garnish

Chop the onion finely and slice the carrots wafer thin. Sautez in half the butter until they are soft and golden. Add the wine and stock to the pan, together with the bouquet garni, salt and pepper. Simmer for a few minutes.

Take the scallops from their shells and wash well in running water. Add to the pan and poach very gently for 7 or 8 minutes without allowing the cooking liquid to boil. Remove the scallops and vegetables to a serving dish and keep warm. Strain the cooking liquor, reduce to about ¼ pt (150 ml, *generous ½ cup*) and whisk in the cream and the remaining butter. Pour the sauce over the dish and garnish with the finely chopped herbs.

Coquilles St Jacques Bonne Femme

8–12 scallops, according to size
2–3 shallots
2 oz (50 g) butter
4 oz (100 g) mushrooms
2 tbs parsley
¼ pt (150 ml) non-vintage champagne
¼ pt (150 ml) fish stock (see p21)
¼ pt (150 ml) double or whipping cream or *crème fraîche*
salt, pepper

8–10 sea scallops, according to size
2–3 shallots
4 tbs (½ stick) butter
¼ lb mushrooms
2 tbs parsley
generous ½ cup non-vintage champagne
generous ½ cup fish stock (see p21)
generous ½ cup heavy cream or crème fraîche
salt, pepper

Chop the shallots finely and soften in half the butter. Add the finely sliced mushrooms and cook for a further 5–10 minutes. Take the scallops out of their shells and wash well in cold running water. Cut them into pieces and add to the vegetables, together with the chopped parsley. Sautez lightly. Add the champagne and the stock, cover, and cook fast for 4 minutes. Strain off the scallops and the vegetables and divide between four individual heatproof dishes.

Reduce the cooking liquor, if necessary, to ¼ pt (150 ml, *generous ½ cup*). Add the cream and reduce again. Enrich the sauce by whisking in the rest of the butter, cut into small pieces, and correct the seasoning. Pour the sauce over the scallops and glaze under a hot grill. Serve immediately.

Gratin de Fruits de Mer

If it is impossible to find *écrevisses* (crayfish) for this marvellous dish, then use *langoustines* or Dublin Bay prawns. The taste will be as good, but the sauce will not be quite such a pretty pink colour. The quantity of olive oil and cognac or *marc de champagne* may seem enormous, but there are a lot of crayfish to *sauter* and *flamber*.

2½ quarts (3 l) mussels	*5 lb mussels*
20 scallops	*20 sea scallops*
8 oz (225 g) shelled shrimps	*½ lb shelled shrimps*
2 lb (1 kg) monkfish or any firm-fleshed white fish	*2 lb angler fish (belly fish) or any firm-fleshed white fish*
8 fillets of sole	*8 fillets of sole*
½ bottle non-vintage champagne	*½ bottle non-vintage champagne*
1 pt (½ l) fish stock (see p21)	*2½ cups fish stock (see p21)*

Sauce de Coulis d'Ecrevisses: *Sauce de Coulis d'Ecrevisses:*

20 crayfish (or 40 *langoustines* or Dublin Bay prawns)	*20 crayfish (or 40 jumbo shrimps)*
¾ pt (425 ml) olive oil	*1¾ cups olive oil*
⅓ pt (200 ml) cognac or *marc de champagne*	*1 cup cognac or Calvados*
2 onions	*2 onions*
1 carrot	*1 carrot*
2 tbs tomato purée	*2 tbs tomato paste*
1 lb (450 g) tomatoes	*1 lb tomatoes*
bouquet garni	*bouquet garni*
1½ pt (850 ml) Saran or dry white wine	*3½ cups Saran or dry white wine*
½ pt (300 ml) double or whipping cream or *crème fraîche*	*1¼ cups heavy cream or crème fraîche*
salt, pepper	*salt, pepper*

Start by making the sauce, as this has to cook for a long time. The fish can be prepared while the sauce is simmering.

Sauce de Coulis d'Ecrevisses: Remove the meat from the crayfish or prawn tails and put on one side. Put all the shells, heads, etc., in a pan and sautez in olive oil. Flame with the cognac or *marc de champagne* (*Calvados*). Add the onions and carrot, thinly sliced, cover, and sweat for 5 minutes. Add the tomato purée (*paste*) and the tomatoes cut in quarters, cover, and sweat again for 10–15 minutes. Add the bouquet garni, pour in the white wine and season. Simmer for 1½ hours with the lid off.

Remove from the stove and sieve, crushing the shells very hard to obtain as much purée as possible from the fish and vegetables. Return to the pan. Reduce the sauce at least to half or until it starts to look shiny and bubbles thickly. Add the cream and reduce again.

To prepare the fish: Wash and clean the mussels and open over a high flame in the champagne. Take out and reserve. Poach the scallops in the champagne cooking liquor. Take out and reserve. Next poach the meat from the crayfish tails which you have reserved from the sauce, remove and put on one side. Poach the shrimps and set on one side. Cut the monkfish (*angler fish*) and the fillets of sole into bite-sized pieces and poach in the fish stock. Drain and reserve. Arrange all the fish in a gratin dish and keep warm. Strain the champagne cooking liquor into the *Sauce de Coulis* and reduce a little more if necessary.

When everything is ready, pour the sauce over the fish and glaze briefly under a salamander or grill.

Bar au Fenouil
(Sea Bass with Fennel)

1½ lb (675 g) sea bass fillets	*1½ lb sea bass fillets*
2 onions	*2 onions*
about 4 tbs olive oil	*about 4 tbs olive oil*
about 5 oz (125 g) butter	*scant ¾ cup (1¼ sticks) butter*
3–4 fennel 'bulbs'	*3–4 fennel 'bulbs'*
bouquet garni	*bouquet garni*
⅔ pt (350 ml) dry white wine	*1½ cups dry white wine*
salt, pepper, cayenne pepper	*salt, pepper, cayenne pepper*

Chop the onions finely and gently sweat them in about 2 tbs olive oil and 1 oz (25 g, *2 tbs*) butter. When they are golden add the finely sliced fennel, the bouquet garni and the wine. Season, cover the pan and simmer very gently for 1–1½ hours, until the vegetables are quite soft. Meanwhile chop the fennel green finely and put on one side.

Grill the bass, or bake in a moderate oven, covered with foil, for 20–25 minutes with a little butter and oil. Arrange on a serving dish and keep warm.

Drain the onion and fennel well – reserving the cooking liquor – and purée them. Mix in a nut (*pat*) of butter and put in a separate serving dish. Keep warm.

Cut the remaining butter (about 2 oz, *4 tbs*) into dice. In a small pan put 2 tbs water and the reserved cooking liquor, and reduce until about 1½ tbs remains. Off the heat, beat in 2 pieces of the butter. Return the pan to a low heat and continue to add the butter, a piece at a time, vigorously whisking in each piece as you add it, until the sauce is thick and smooth. Do not let the sauce separate or all you will have is melted butter. Add the chopped fennel green and some cayenne pepper, and a little salt if necessary. Pour the sauce over the fish.

Bar en Bellevue
(Sea Bass with Mayonnaise)

1 sea bass weighing $3\frac{1}{2}$–4 lb ($1\frac{3}{4}$–2 kg)
$\frac{1}{2}$ pt (300 ml) mayonnaise
1 tbs port
3 tbs chopped chervil and parsley
yolks of 2 hard-boiled eggs
salt, pepper

Court-bouillon:

5 pt ($2\frac{1}{2}$ l) water
3 carrots, sliced
1 onion, sliced
bouquet garni
12 peppercorns
1 tbs salt
juice of 2 lemons

Garnishes: see below

1 sea bass weighing $3\frac{1}{2}$–4 lb
$1\frac{1}{4}$ cups mayonnaise
1 tbs port
3 tbs chopped chervil and parsley
yolks of 2 hard-boiled eggs
salt, pepper

Court-bouillon:

12 cups water
3 carrots, sliced
1 onion, sliced
bouquet garni
12 peppercorns
1 tbs salt
juice of 2 lemons

Garnishes: see below

Make the *court-bouillon* first. Put all the ingredients into a large pan, bring to the boil and simmer, uncovered, for 15–20 minutes. Strain.

Poach the fish gently in this stock for 30–35 minutes or until cooked through. Allow it to cool in the cooking liquid.

Add the port and herbs to the mayonnaise, season, and garnish with the chopped hard-boiled egg-yolks.

Strain the fish well, skin it and transfer to a serving dish. Garnish in one of the ways described below. Serve the mayonnaise separately.

Garnishes:

1. Pieces of cucumber, hollowed out and stuffed with a mixture of tuna fish and mayonnaise.
2. Halved hard-boiled eggs, the yolks mixed with mayonnaise and a little chopped truffle.
3. Lettuce hearts, parsley sprigs, slices of lemon and tomatoes.

Gâteau de Turbotin aux Epinards
(Turbot with Spinach)

1½ lb (675 g) small turbot or brill
   fillets
1 lb (450 g) spinach
3–4 tbs double or whipping
   cream or *crème fraîche*
about ½ pt (300 ml) fish stock
   (see p21)

1½ lb small flounder or fluke fillets
1 lb spinach
4–5 tbs heavy cream or crème
   fraîche
about 1¼ cups fish stock (see p21)

Mousseline:
10 oz (275 g) whiting flesh
1 small egg-white
5–6 tbs double or whipping
   cream or *crème fraîche*
salt

Mousseline:
10 oz whiting flesh
1 small egg-white
6–7 tbs heavy cream or crème
   fraîche
salt

Béchamel sauce:
1½ oz (40 g) butter
1 oz (25 g) flour
½ pt (275 ml) milk
½ pt (275 ml) double or whipping
   cream or *crème fraîche*
nut of butter
salt, pepper, nutmeg, cayenne

Béchamel sauce:
3 tbs butter
2 tbs flour
1¼ cups milk
1¼ cups heavy cream or crème
   fraîche
pat of butter
salt, pepper, nutmeg, cayenne

Make 3 shallow cuts in the skin side of each fillet and beat gently on both sides to prevent them from curling up at the edges.

Wash the spinach well. Fill a large pan with water, bring it to the boil and put in the spinach. As soon as the water comes to the boil again drain the spinach and refresh in cold water. Press well to extract all the moisture, and chop roughly. Heat gently in a small pan with the cream, warming the two together without cooking the spinach. Leave to cool.

Next make the *mousseline.*

Mousseline: Chop the whiting flesh into small pieces and cream in a food processor. Add salt and the egg-white. Slowly add enough cream to make a thickish, spreadable purée – it should not be runny. If you haven't a food processor rub the whiting flesh through a fine sieve or put it twice through the fine blade of a mincer, and beat in the egg-white and the cream so that the *mousseline* is perfectly smooth.

To assemble: Spread some of the mousseline on each of the larger fillets, followed by a layer of spinach. Put the smaller fillets on top and cover with another layer of mousseline. Arrange in one layer in an ovenproof dish and pour over the fish stock, which should come about halfway up the bottom fillet. Cover with well-buttered greaseproof paper and put in a fairly hot oven (400°F, 200°C, gas mark 6) for about 30 minutes, or until the fish is cooked through. While it is cooking, make the *béchamel* sauce.

Béchamel sauce: Melt the butter and add the flour, stirring for 3 or 4 minutes without letting it colour. Add the hot milk all at once, stirring vigorously until the sauce is smooth. Season with salt and pepper, a shake of cayenne pepper and a little nutmeg. Add the cream and stir in the nut (*pat*) of butter chopped into 2 or 3 pieces. If you are preparing the dish in advance, leave the sauce in a covered basin in a *bain-marie* until you are ready to use it.

When the fish is cooked, take it out of the dish, being careful to strain it well, and arrange in a shallow ovenproof serving dish. Pour the sauce all over it and put under a hot grill for a few moments to glaze.

Turbot Maître d'Hôtel Braisé au Saran   Serves 4
(Braised Turbot with Maître d'Hôtel Butter)

If small turbot are not available, brill will do excellently instead. They normally weigh about 1½ lb, so for 4 people you will need two.

4 small turbot, weighing ¾–1 lb (350–450 g) each	*4 small flounder or fluke, weighing ¾–1 lb each*
8 oz (225 g) butter	*generous 1 cup (2 sticks) butter*
6 tbs chopped parsley	*8 tbs chopped parsley*
1–1½ lemons	*1–1½ lemons*
8 oz (225 g) shallots	*½ lb shallots*
1 pt (½ l) Ruinart Chardonnay or dry white wine	*2½ cups Ruinart Chardonnay or dry white wine*
salt, pepper	*salt, pepper*

Remove the head and the dark skin and loosen the fillets from the backbone. Soften three-quarters of the butter and into this beat most of the chopped parsley, with salt, pepper and lemon juice to taste. Spread a pat of this butter under each fillet, and lay the fish, overlapping, on a bed of finely chopped shallots in a shallow dish. Pour over the wine and the juice of ½ lemon. Season. Cover the fish and cook in a moderate oven (350°F, 180°C, gas mark 4) until the fish is tender (30–40 minutes). Remove the fish to a serving dish and keep warm.

Strain the cooking liquor into a pan and reduce by half, or until it has thickened considerably. Whisk in the remaining butter, cut into small pieces. When the sauce is perfectly smooth pour it over the fish. Serve sprinkled with the remaining chopped parsley.

Colin Provençale
(Hake Baked with Tomatoes)

3 lb (1.35 kg) hake in one piece	*3 lb hake in one piece*
1 lb (450 g) onions	*1 lb onions*
1 clove garlic	*1 clove garlic*
1½–2 lb (675 g–1 kg) tomatoes	*1½–2 lb tomatoes*
olive oil	*olive oil*
butter	*butter*
salt, pepper	*salt, pepper*

Skin the fish and wash it well under running cold water. Chop the onions finely and crush the garlic clove. Peel and de-pip (*seed*) the tomatoes, squeeze out the juice and roughly chop the flesh. Gently cook the onions, garlic and tomato in a little olive oil in a covered pan, seasoning with salt and pepper, until they are quite soft.

Put the fish in a baking pan just large enough to hold it, and spread the onion and tomato mixture all over it. Add a few knobs of butter, cover the pan well with a buttered greaseproof paper and cook in a fairly hot oven (400°F, 200°C, gas mark 6) for about 50 minutes, until the fish is cooked right through.

Remove to a serving dish, being careful not to disturb the coating of vegetable mixture. Reduce the cooking liquid a little and pour it over before serving.

If hake is not available, cod can be used instead for this appetising dish.

Colin Concombres aux Fines Herbes
(Hake with Cucumber and *Fines Herbes*)

Serves 4

4 hake steaks each 7–8 oz (225 g)	*4 hake or halibut steaks each 7–8 oz*
2 large cucumbers	*2 large cucumbers*
butter for frying	*butter for frying*
	Beurre Blanc
Beurre Fondu aux Fines Herbes	*Beurre Fondu aux Fines Herbes:*
2 tbs non-vintage champagne or dry white wine	*2 tbs non-vintage champagne or dry white wine*
6 oz (150 g) very cold butter	*¾ cup (1½ sticks) very cold butter*
2–3 tbs finely chopped *fines herbes* or parsley	*2–3 tbs finely chopped fines herbes or parsley*
salt	*salt*

Fry the hake steaks in butter.

While they are cooking, skin the cucumbers and cut into pieces about 2½″ (6 cm) long. Trim the pieces into the shape of olives and blanch for 10 minutes to remove the bitterness and soften them. Sautez gently in butter in a separate pan.

Arrange the fish on a serving dish and surround with the cucumber olives. Keep warm while you make the *Beurre Fondu.*

Beurre Fondu aux Fines Herbes: Put 1 tbs water and the champagne or white wine in a small pan, with a little salt, and boil for a few minutes until there is about a tablespoon of liquid left. Over a low heat add the butter in small pieces: it must be very firm and cold. Stir briskly with a wire whisk as you add it, and when it is smooth and creamy add the finely chopped *fines herbes* or parsley. Serve separately.

Rougets dans leur Nage

(Red Mullet with Sauce Hollandaise) — *Serves 6*

6 medium red mullet	*6 medium red mullet or red snapper*
Court-bouillon:	*Court-bouillon:*
6 oz (150 g) carrots	*6 oz carrots*
6 oz (150 g) onions	*6 oz onions*
6 oz (150 g) leeks	*6 oz leeks*
6 oz (150 g) fennel 'bulb'	*6 oz fennel 'bulb'*
bouquet garni	*bouquet garni*
2½ pt (1½ l) water	*6 cups water*
salt, pepper	*salt, pepper*
Sauce Hollandaise:	*Sauce Hollandaise:*
8 oz (225 g) clarified butter	*½ lb clarified butter*
3 egg-yolks	*3 egg-yolks*
1 teasp lemon juice	*1 teasp lemon juice*
salt	*salt*
parsley for garnish	*parsley for garnish*

Court-bouillon: Put the finely sliced vegetables, the bouquet garni and the water into a pan. Season, bring to the boil, skim, and simmer uncovered for 30 minutes. Allow to cool slightly.

Gently simmer the mullet in the *court-bouillon* for 10–15 minutes, watching to see that the fish doesn't cook too much. Lift it out, put on a serving dish and keep warm. Drain the vegetables, and arrange a few of them neatly on the fish. Garnish with chopped parsley, and serve the *Sauce Hollandaise* separately.

Sauce Hollandaise: This can be prepared while the fish is cooking, or made in advance and left in a warm place in a *bain-marie* until you are ready.

Melt the clarified butter but do not let it get hot. Put the egg-yolks in a basin with 1 tbs water. Set over a pan of hot, but not boiling, water and whisk vigorously until the mixture thickens. Remove from the heat and very gradually add the clarified butter, beating hard all the time. When the sauce is thick and creamy add the lemon juice and a little salt.

Lotte aux Ecrevisses et au Brut Impérial *Serves 6*
(Monkfish with Crayfish in Champagne)

Monkfish, an excellent and economical fish, is popular in France, where chefs and housewives are willing to take trouble with its preparation. Luckily it is gradually gaining popularity elsewhere, too, as people begin to recognise its merits. Any firm-fleshed white fish can be substituted for this dish if monkfish is not available, but the flavour will not be so delicate.

1½ lb (675 g) fillets of monkfish or any firm-fleshed white fish
6 crayfish or about 12 prawns
3 shallots
⅓ pt (200 ml) non-vintage champagne or dry white wine
8 oz (225 g) button mushrooms
5 ripe tomatoes
parsley and chervil, or parsley alone
about 4 oz (100 g) butter
2 tbs oil
a little saffron
⅓ pt (200 ml) fish stock (see p21)
⅓ pt (200 ml) double or whipping cream or *crème fraîche*
salt, pepper

1½ lb fillets of angler fish, belly fish, or any firm-fleshed white fish
6 crayfish or about 12 jumbo shrimps
3 shallots
1 cup non-vintage champagne or dry white wine
½ lb button mushrooms
5 ripe tomatoes
parsley and chervil, or parsley alone
generous ½ cup (1 stick) butter
2 tbs oil
a little saffron
1 cup fish stock (see p21)
1 cup heavy cream or crème fraîche
salt, pepper

Cut the fish into steaks about ½″ (1 cm) thick and season them with a little pepper but no salt. Chop the shallots very finely and soak them in a tablespoon or two of the champagne or wine. Slice the mushrooms, not too finely. Peel and de-pip (*seed*) the tomatoes and chop them fairly coarsely. Chop the parsley and chervil. Shell the crayfish or prawns (*shrimps*).

Put a generous knob of butter and the oil in a pan, add the shallots and soften gently without allowing them to brown. Add the mushrooms, most of the parsley and chervil (keeping a little for garnish), the tomatoes, and a little saffron infused in a spoonful or two of hot stock. Place the fish on top, add the champagne or dry white wine and the fish stock, cover the pan, and leave to simmer for 5–8 minutes, turning the fish halfway through. When the fish is cooked remove it to a serving dish. Strain the vegetables and arrange them on top of the fish. Keep warm.

Return the cooking liquor to the pan and reduce until thick and bubbly. Stir in the cream and reduce again, finally incorporating a knob of butter. Meanwhile gently simmer the crayfish or prawns for a few minutes in fish stock or water. Strain into the sauce any juice from the dish on which the fish is being kept warm – this is important, as the flesh of the monkfish is quite watery, and the excess moisture may make the sauce too thin. Test the sauce for seasoning, and reduce again if necessary.

Arrange the crayfish or prawns round the fish, and pour the sauce over it. Sprinkle with the rest of the chopped parsley.

Salon du Trianon

Filet de Boeuf Tante Nicole	(Fillet of Beef with Onions and Tomatoes)
Filet de Boeuf en Croûte	(Fillet of Beef in Pastry)
Boeuf Braisé à la Mode de Chez Nous	(Beef Braised in Red Wine)
Roulade des Vendangeurs	(Beef Olives Cooked in Red Wine)
Grenadins de Veau 'A. Desvignes'	
Foie de Veau Braisé au Madère	(Calf's Liver Braised in Madeira)
Ris de Veau Charentais	(Sweetbreads with Mushroom and Tomato Sauce)
Ris de Veau Braisés au Confit de Poireaux	(Braised Sweetbreads with Leeks)
Carré d'Agneau au Champagne	(Loin of Lamb with Champagne)
Gigot Braisé à l'Estragon	(Braised Leg of Lamb with Tarragon)
Ballotine d'Agneau Braisé	(Stuffed Shoulder of Lamb)
Rôti de Porc à la Sultane	(Roast Loin of Pork with Rice)
Carré de Porc – Pommes 'en l'Air'	(Loin of Pork with Apples)
Jambon Braisé au Champagne	(Ham Braised in Champagne)
Rognons de Veau au Brut Impérial	(Veal Kidneys Cooked in Champagne)
Croûte aux Rognons	(Kidneys on Toast)
Potée Champenoise	

Filet de Boeuf Tante Nicole

(Fillet of Beef with Onions and Tomatoes)

2 lb (1 kg) fillet of beef	*2 lb fillet of beef*
pork fat back for barding	*pork fat back for barding*
2 lb (1 kg) button onions	*2 lb button onions (small white)*
about 3 oz (75 g) butter	*scant ½ cup (¾ stick) butter*
12 small tomatoes	*12 small tomatoes*
4 oz (100 g) bacon	*¼ lb bacon*
1 truffle (optional)	*1 truffle (optional)*
salt, pepper, sugar	*salt, pepper, sugar*

Trim the fillet, removing all the fat and sinews. Season, and wrap in the pork fat back. Put in a baking pan and roast in a hot oven (450°F, 230°C, gas mark 8) for about 30 minutes, keeping it pink.

Meanwhile, in a covered pan, gently cook the onions in about two-thirds of the butter, with a little salt and pepper and sugar, until they are soft (this will take about 25 minutes). Peel the tomatoes and add them, whole, to the onions for a few minutes towards the end of the cooking time, until they too are soft, but do not let them lose their shape. Cut the bacon *julienne*, slice the truffle, and cook together in the rest of the butter.

Remove the meat to a serving dish and arrange the onions and tomatoes round it. Put the bacon and truffle on top, and pour over it the juice from the roasting pan.

Filet de Boeuf en Croûte
(Fillet of Beef in Pastry)

At the Royal Champagne the beef is wrapped in brioche dough. But this calls for high technique, and even very experienced chefs sometimes find it a bit tricky and unpredictable, so we felt that it would be more helpful to substitute puff pastry. However, for those who want to try the real thing, the recipe for the brioche is given on page 26.

This dish should be accompanied by a Truffle Sauce (*Sauce Périgueux*), but a less extravagant alternative is a good mushroom sauce.

3½ lb (1½ kg) fillet of beef
1½ lb (675 g) puff pastry
1 oz (25 g) butter
wash of egg-yolk and a little milk
salt, pepper

3½ lb fillet of beef
1½ lb puff pastry
2 tbs (¼ stick) butter
wash of egg-yolk and a little milk
salt, pepper

Sauce Périgueux or Mushroom Sauce:

2–3 truffles *or* 12 oz (350 g) mushrooms and 1 oz (25 g) butter
1 oz (25 g) lard
2 teasp oil
2 oz (50 g) streaky bacon
1 carrot
1 celery stalk
1 tbs cornflour
1½ pt (850 ml) beef stock
2 teasp tomato purée
bouquet garni
6 tbs (100 ml) Madeira
salt, pepper

Sauce Périgueux or Mushroom Sauce:

2–3 truffles or ¾ lb mushrooms and 2 tbs (¼ stick) butter
2 tbs lard
2 teasp oil
2 oz bacon
1 carrot
1 celery stalk
1 tbs cornstarch
3½ cups beef stock
2 teasp tomato paste
bouquet garni
7 tbs (generous ⅓ cup) Madeira
salt, pepper

Trim the beef, removing all fat and sinews. Heat the butter in a large frying pan and brown the fillet on all sides, seasoning with salt and pepper. If you like the meat *à point* (*medium rare*), it should be partly roasted at this stage. In any case, leave it to cool completely.

Roll out the puff pastry to a neat shape which will comfortably hold the beef. Place the meat in the middle and fold the pastry over it lengthwise so that there is a neat join along the top. Press the edges together with a little water. Secure each end with a similar join along the top. Brush with the milk and egg-yolk wash and bake in a hot oven (450°F, 230°C, gas mark 8) for about 45 minutes. You can tell when the meat is done by sticking a small, sharp-pointed knife into the centre and touching it against your lips: if you like the meat rare, it is 'done' when the knife is lukewarm, but if you like it *à point* the knife should be hot.

Sauce Périgueux or *Mushroom Sauce:* Start to make the sauce before you put the meat in the oven. Melt the lard and oil in a saucepan and add the bacon, derinded and chopped, the diced carrot and the chopped celery stalk. Fry gently for 8–10 minutes. Add the cornflour (*cornstarch*) and stir until it is a light brown. Remove from the heat and gradually add the hot stock, stirring well. Return to the heat and continue to stir until the sauce thickens and is quite smooth. Add the bouquet garni, the tomato purée (*paste*) and seasoning. Cover and simmer gently for at least 30 minutes. Remove the bouquet garni and rub the sauce through a sieve.

Slice the truffles thinly and combine with the Madeira in a small pan. Simmer gently until the wine has reduced by half and add to the sauce.

If you are substituting mushrooms for the truffles, slice them thinly and put them in a small pan with the butter. Cook for a few minutes, shaking the pan from time to time. Add to the sauce, simmer for 5 minutes and add the Madeira.

Heat the sauce well, but don't let it boil or the flavour of the wine will be lost.

The sauce should be served separately.

Boeuf Braisé à la Mode de Chez Nous
(Beef Braised in Red Wine)

Serves 8–10

4–5 lb (about 2 kg) chuck
   steak in one piece
2 oz (50 g) butter
mushroom stalks
1 calf's foot, cut in two
salt, pepper

Marinade:
1¾ pt (1 l) red wine
2 carrots
2 onions
2 cloves garlic
1 bayleaf
fresh thyme

4–5 lb chuck steak in one piece
4 tbs (½ stick) butter
mushroom stalks
1 calf's foot, cut in two
salt, pepper

Marinade:
4 cups red wine
2 carrots
2 onions
2 cloves garlic
1 bayleaf
fresh thyme

Ideally, the beef for this dish should be larded. If your butcher will do this for you, so much the better; if you want to do it for yourself, one method is described on page 25. Even in the best French kitchens, however, larding seems gradually to be disappearing, and this is an excellent dish without it.

Roll the beef and tie it if necessary. Season and put in a bowl just large enough to hold it. Cover with the marinade.

Marinade: Chop the carrots and onions fairly finely and spread them over the meat, together with the unpeeled garlic cloves, the bayleaf and the fresh thyme. Pour the wine over the top and leave for at least 6 hours, turning from time to time.

When you are ready to cook the meat, take it out of the marinading liquid and dry it thoroughly. Colour it on all sides in the butter in a heavy casserole into which the meat just fits. Add the marinade, the mushroom stalks and the calf's foot, cut in two. Season. Cover closely and braise in a fairly hot oven (400°F, 200°C, gas mark 6) for 3½–4 hours. It should remain at a gentle simmer, so adjust the oven heat if necessary. Baste from time to time.

When the meat is done, remove from the casserole and keep warm. Remove the calf's foot and liquidise or strain the cooking liquor, pressing through as much of the vegetables as possible. Return to the casserole and reheat, reducing if necessary.

The meat can either be carved before serving, with a little of the sauce poured on and the rest handed round separately, or it can be served in one piece. In the latter case, place it on an ovenproof dish, spoon some of the sauce over the top and put it in a very hot oven to glaze. Repeat this process until the meat is quite shiny.

Serve with an accompaniment of glazed carrots and onions.

Roulade des Vendangeurs   *Serves 6*
(Beef Olives Cooked in Red Wine)

about 2 lb (1 kg) topside or silverside, cut into very thin slices
8 oz (225 g) cooked ham, very thinly sliced
8 oz (225 g) sausage meat
1 onion
butter ⎱ for frying
olive oil ⎰
8 oz (225 g) mushrooms
1 pt (½ l) Bouzy or good red wine
6 eggs
salt, pepper

about 2 lb topside (top round), cut into very thin slices
½ lb cooked ham, very thinly sliced
½ lb sausage meat
1 onion
butter ⎱ *for frying*
olive oil ⎰
½ lb mushrooms
2½ cups Bouzy or good red wine
6 eggs
salt, pepper

Chop the onion finely and cook gently in a little butter until it is soft but not brown. Chop the mushrooms finely and add them to the pan. Continue to cook for 5 minutes or so or until the mushrooms are soft. Mix with the sausage meat and season.

Trim the slices of beef and beat until they are as thin as possible. On each piece put a slice of ham and a little of the sausage mixture. Roll up and tie with thin string or thread. Fry lightly on all sides in butter and olive oil and transfer to a casserole. Add the Bouzy or red wine to the frying pan and bring to the boil. Pour over the *roulades*, cover the pan and cook in a medium oven (350°F, 175°C, gas mark 4) for about 1 hour, or until the beef is tender.

Take the *roulades* out of the casserole and remove the string. Arrange on a serving dish and keep warm. Strain the cooking liquor into a pan, reduce rapidly until it has the consistency of gravy and pour over the *roulades*.

Fry the eggs, arrange them on top and serve at once.

This dish should be accompanied by button (*small white*) onions gently cooked in butter for about 25 minutes.

Grenadins de Veau 'A. Desvignes'   Serves 4

4 grenadins of veal (small fillets
   cut from the leg) about 5 oz
   (125 g) each
2 small veal kidneys
flour
about 4 oz (100 g) butter
½ bottle non-vintage
   champagne
8 oz (225 g) mushrooms
½ oz (15 g) potato flour
3 tbs double or whipping cream
   or *crème fraîche*
a little very good veal stock
salt, pepper

4 grenadins of veal (small fillets
   cut from the leg) about 5 oz each
2 small veal kidneys
flour
generous ½ cup (1 stick) butter
½ bottle non-vintage champagne
½ lb mushrooms
1 tbs potato flour or cornstarch
3 tbs heavy cream or crème fraîche
a little very good veal stock
salt, pepper

Pancakes:

1 small egg
¼ pt (150 ml) milk
2 oz (50 g) flour
2 oz (50 g) raisins
1 cup very strong tea
lard for frying
salt, pepper

Pancakes:

1 small egg
generous ½ cup milk
½ cup flour
½ cup raisins
1 cup very strong tea
lard for frying
salt, pepper

Start by making the pancake mixture:

Pancakes: Beat the egg, milk and flour well together, season, and let the mixture stand for an hour. Steep the raisins in the hot tea to soften them.

Lightly flour the grenadins and season them. In a very hot pan seal them quickly in a little butter. Add three-quarters of the champagne, cover, and cook them over a very low heat for 20 minutes.

Meanwhile gently cook the kidneys in butter. Remove from the pan and keep warm.

When the grenadins are done take them out of the pan and keep warm. Put the mushrooms into the pan and cook them for 5 minutes. Mix the potato flour with a little cold water and stir into the pan, together with a nut (*pat*) of butter, the cream, the rest of the champagne and a little veal stock. Test the seasoning and add the juice from the pan in which the kidneys were cooked.

Strain the raisins and rinse in cold water. Make four pancakes in a 6″ (15 cm) pan, incorporating a quarter of the raisins in each. The pancakes should be a little thicker than usual.

Arrange the grenadins on a serving dish and cover with the very hot sauce. On each grenadin lay a half-kidney, finally covering with a pancake, folded in half.

Foie de Veau Braisé au Madère   *Serves 6*
(Calf's Liver Braised in Madeira)

2 lb (1 kg) calf's liver in one piece	2 lb calf's liver in one piece
a very thin slice of pork fat back (6–7 oz, 150–200 g)	a very thin slice of pork fat back (6–7 oz)
a little oil	a little oil
1 onion	1 onion
1 carrot	1 carrot
2 cloves garlic	2 cloves garlic
thyme	thyme
1 bayleaf	1 bayleaf
⅓ pt (200 ml) white wine	1 cup white wine
½ pt (300 ml) Madeira	1¼ cups Madeira
3 oz (75 g) butter	scant ½ cup (¾ stick) butter
salt, pepper	salt, pepper

Season the liver and wrap it in the pork fat, tying it into a neat parcel with fine string. In a casserole, heat the oil and colour the 'parcel' on all sides. Remove from the pan. Chop the onion and carrot, crush the garlic, and add to the pan with a few sprigs of thyme and the bayleaf. Allow the vegetables to sweat. Deglaze the pan with the wine, and when this is very well reduced add the Madeira. Return the meat to the pan. Lower the heat and cook gently, covered, for about 20 minutes, basting from time to time (the liver should still be pink when cooked). Take out the meat, discard the pork fat, and keep the liver warm.

Skim off any fat from the cooking liquor, and strain. Return to the pan, reduce a little if necessary, and enrich by whisking in the butter in small pieces.

Slice the liver, arrange on a serving dish and pour the sauce over the top.

If you have any left over, whisk it in the mixer next day and serve cold as pâté – it is delicious.

Ris de Veau Charentais
(Sweetbreads with Mushroom and Tomato Sauce)

Serves 5

2¼ lb (1 kg) sweetbreads (calf's or lamb's)
1 onion
12 oz (350 g) tomatoes
6 oz (150 g) mushrooms
¼ pt (150 ml) white stock
¼ pt (150 ml) dry white wine
3 oz (75 g) truffles (optional)
2 oz (50 g) butter
4 oz (100 g) cooked ham
¼ pt (150 ml) double or whipping cream or *crème fraîche*
salt, pepper
croûtons to garnish

2¼ lb calf's sweetbreads
1 onion
¾ lb tomatoes
6 oz mushrooms
generous ½ cup white stock
generous ½ cup dry white wine
3 oz truffles (optional)
4 tbs (½ stick) butter
¼ lb cooked ham
generous ½ cup heavy cream or crème fraîche
salt, pepper
croûtons to garnish

Soak the sweetbreads in cold water for at least 2–3 hours, changing the water frequently. Blanch by bringing them slowly to the boil in salted water. Skim, drain, and refresh in cold water. Remove the sinews – the rubbery bits attached to the meat – and as much of the membranes as will easily come away. Press between two plates or chopping boards with a heavy weight on top until you are ready to cook.

Put the sweetbreads in a shallow casserole with the sliced onion, the chopped tomatoes, two-thirds of the mushrooms, chopped, the stock, the wine, a pinch of salt and a little pepper. Cover with foil and cook in a moderate oven (350°F, 180°C, gas mark 4) until tender – about 45 minutes.

While the sweetbreads are cooking slice the remaining mushrooms and the truffles, if you are using them, and toss in butter. When nearly cooked add the ham, sliced *julienne*, and warm through.

When the sweetbreads are ready remove them from the casserole, slice them, arrange on a serving dish and keep warm. Sieve or liquidise the vegetables and the cooking liquor, return to the pan, reduce by half and stir in the cream.

Cover the sweetbreads with this sauce, sprinkle with the mushrooms, truffles and ham, and decorate with croûtons fried in butter.

Ris de Veau Braisés au Confit de Poireaux   *Serves 6*
(Braised Sweetbreads with Leeks)

(thymus gland)

2¼ lb (1 kg) calf's sweetbreads	*2¼ lb calf's sweetbreads*
(or lamb's can be used)	*¾ cup (1½ sticks) butter*
6 oz (175 g) butter	*1 carrot*
1 carrot	*1 onion*
1 onion	*2 cloves garlic*
2 cloves garlic	*bouquet garni*
bouquet garni	*1½ cups dry white wine*
⅔ pt (350 ml) dry white wine	*1 lb leeks*
1 lb (450 g) leeks	*generous ½ cup heavy cream or*
¼ pt (150 ml) double cream or	*crème fraîche*
crème fraîche	*salt, pepper*
salt, pepper	*chervil to garnish*
chervil to garnish	

Soak the sweetbreads in cold water for at least 2 to 3 hours, changing the water frequently. Blanch by bringing them slowly to the boil in salted water. Skim, drain and refresh in cold water. Remove the sinews – the rubbery pieces attached to the meat – and as much of the membranes as will easily come away. Press between two plates or chopping boards with a heavy weight on top until ready to cook.

Melt a third of the butter in a shallow casserole and sweat the chopped carrot, onion and garlic with the bouquet garni. When the vegetables are soft lay the sweetbreads on top. Add the wine, season lightly, cover and cook in a moderate oven (350°F, 180°C, gas mark 4) for about 40 minutes.

While the sweetbreads are cooking finely chop the leeks and cook gently to make a 'compote' in half the remaining butter, a little water and salt and pepper. When the liquid has all but evaporated and the leeks are soft, mix in half the cream.

When the sweetbreads are cooked, drain and keep warm. Strain the cooking liquor, pressing through a little of the vegetables, return to the pan and reduce by about half. Whisk in the remaining butter and the rest of the cream, and reduce again to the consistency of thinnish cream. Slice the sweetbreads and arrange on a serving dish, surround with the leeks, pour over the sauce and scatter with chopped chervil.

93

Carré d'Agneau au Champagne *Serves 4–5*
(Loin of Lamb with Champagne)

2½–3 lb (1¼ kg) loin of lamb
3–4 oz (75–100 g) butter
3 onions
2 carrots
12 peppercorns
bouquet garni
1 tbs tomato purée
½ bottle non-vintage champagne
½ pt (300 ml) veal stock
3–4 tbs oil
5 oz (125 g) fresh breadcrumbs
3 shallots
6 tbs chopped parsley
salt, pepper

2½–3 lb loin of lamb
about ½ cup (¾–1 stick) butter
3 onions
2 carrots
12 peppercorns
bouquet garni
1 tbs tomato paste
½ bottle non-vintage champagne
1¼ cups veal stock
4–5 tbs oil
about 2 cups fresh breadcrumbs
3 shallots
7 tbs chopped parsley
salt, pepper

Ask your butcher for one or two lamb bones and some trimmings, to enrich the sauce.

Start by making this sauce, as it cooks for a long time. Put the bones and trimmings into a sauté pan with a little of the butter, and brown them well. Add the onions and carrots, roughly chopped, the peppercorns, the bouquet garni and the tomato purée (*paste*), and cook gently for a few minutes. Skim off the fat and deglaze with the champagne. Transfer the contents of the pan to a fireproof casserole and add the stock. Season, cover the pan and simmer gently for 2½ hours.

Meanwhile, roast the lamb with the oil and a little butter. Set the oven to hot (450°F, 230°C, gas mark 8) for the first 20–30 minutes, so that the meat will brown, then lower to (350°F, 180°C, gas mark 4) for the rest of the cooking time – about 1¼ hours in all. Mix together very thoroughly the breadcrumbs, the finely chopped shallots and the chopped parsley. Season. When the lamb is done transfer it to an ovenproof dish and cover it thickly with this mixture, pressing it firmly into the meat. Leave in a warm place for 15 minutes.

Take the bones and the trimmings out of the sauce and strain, pressing through as much of the vegetables as you can. Skim off the fat from the pan in which the lamb was cooked and add the cooking liquor to the sauce. Reduce a little if necessary.

When you are ready to eat the lamb put it under a salamander or a very hot grill for a few minutes to brown the breadcrumb mixture. Serve the sauce separately.

Gigot Braisé à l'Estragon
(Braised Leg of Lamb with Tarragon)

In North America a 4½ lb leg of lamb is available only during March and April. The rest of the year it will weigh 6–8 lb, and will then feed at least 8 to 10 people, depending on the rest of the menu.

leg of lamb weighing about
   4½ lb (2 kg)
6–8 sprigs fresh tarragon
2 tbs oil
1 oz (25 g) butter
1 carrot
3 onions
10 peppercorns
1 small calf's foot
bouquet garni
2 cloves garlic
1 tbs tomato purée
1 bottle Coteaux Champenois or
   dry white wine
½–¾ pt (300–425 ml) white
   stock
salt, pepper

leg of lamb weighing about 4½ lb
6–8 sprigs fresh tarragon
2 tbs oil
2 tbs (¼ stick) butter
1 carrot
3 onions
10 peppercorns
1 small calf's foot
bouquet garni
2 cloves garlic
1 tbs tomato paste
1 bottle Coteaux Champenois or dry
   white wine
1¼–1¾ cups white stock
salt, pepper

Stuff most of the tarragon between the flesh and bone of the lamb. Brown in a big casserole, in a mixture of oil and butter, until it is golden brown all over. Remove from the pan.

Add to the cooking fat the diced carrot and the quartered onions, the crushed peppercorns, the calf's foot, the bouquet garni (which should include a sprig of tarragon), the unpeeled garlic cloves and the tomato purée (*paste*). Cook for 5 minutes, skim off any fat and add the wine. Season. Return the leg of lamb to the casserole and cook over gentle heat, partially covered, until the cooking liquid has been reduced by about half. Add the same quantity of stock to replace the evaporated wine, cover, and continue cooking over a very gentle heat. The total cooking time is about 3 hours.

Remove the lamb and carve, arranging the slices on a serving dish. Keep warm. Strain the cooking liquid and reduce if necessary. Pour some of it over the meat, serving the rest in a sauceboat. Sprinkle some chopped tarragon over the meat.

A purée of carrots is a good accompaniment to this dish. Boil the sliced carrots in a little salted water until they are soft. Drain, purée, return to the pan, and mix in a little pepper, some butter, a spoonful of cream, and sugar to taste.

Ballotine d'Agneau Braisée
(Stuffed Shoulder of Lamb)

4½ lb (2 kg) shoulder of lamb	*4½ lb shoulder of lamb*
8 oz (225 g) spinach	*½ lb spinach*
3 oz (75 g) mushrooms	*3 oz mushrooms*
2 onions	*2 onions*
about 4 oz (100 g) butter	*generous ½ cup (1 stick) butter*
6 oz (150 g) belly of pork, minced	*6 oz belly of pork, or fatty pork shoulder, minced*
2 oz (50 g) fresh breadcrumbs	*1 generous cup fresh breadcrumbs*
1 egg	*1 egg*
2 tbs cognac	*2 tbs cognac*
handful of basil and parsley, or all parsley	*handful of basil and parsley, or all parsley*
1 calf's foot	*1 calf's foot*
2 sticks celery	*2 stalks celery*
2 carrots	*2 carrots*
⅓ pt (200 ml) Coteaux champenois or dry white wine	*1 cup Coteaux champenois or dry white wine*
⅓ pt (200 ml) veal stock	*1 cup veal stock*
salt, pepper	*salt, pepper*

Ask your butcher to bone the lamb, leaving only the knuckle (this is not necessary, but it looks more stylish, especially if the knuckle is embellished with a paper frill). Open the meat out and flatten it.

Blanch the spinach by plunging it into a large pan of boiling water. Bring the water to the boil again, drain the spinach, and refresh in cold water. Squeeze out all the moisture and spread the spinach over the meat.

Make some *duxelles* of mushrooms by chopping them and squeezing them in a cloth to extract all the moisture. Chop one of the onions finely and brown in a little of the butter. Add the mushrooms and cook briskly until all the liquid has evaporated. Mix with the minced pork and the breadcrumbs, and bind with the beaten egg. Moisten with the cognac and add the chopped parsley and basil, or parsley alone. Season. Lay this stuffing on the meat, roll up and tie securely with string. Colour it on all sides in butter and put into a braising pan with the calf's foot. Chop the celery, the carrots and the remaining onion and sweat in a little butter. Add to the meat, together with the wine and the stock. Cover and cook in a moderate oven (350°F, 180°C, gas mark 4) for about 1½ hours, or until the meat is done. Remove the string from the lamb, place the meat on a serving dish and keep warm.

Strain the cooking liquid and return to the pan. Reduce until it thickens and is strongly flavoured, and enrich with a little butter stirred in. Pour some of it over the lamb and serve the rest separately.

Accompany this dish with *haricots verts*, little tomatoes grilled, sautéed courgettes (*small zucchini or green squash*) and mashed potatoes.

3–3½ lb (1½ kg) loin of pork	*3–3½ lb loin of pork*
2–3 cloves garlic	*2–3 cloves garlic*
1 lb (450 g) button onions	*1 lb button onions (small white)*
6–7 tbs oil	*7–8 tbs oil*
8 oz (225 g) long grain rice	*½ lb long grain rice*
2–3 oz (50–75 g) cooked ham	*2–3 oz cooked ham*
1 onion	*1 onion*
3 tomatoes	*3 tomatoes*
1 tbs tomato purée	*1 tbs tomato paste*
saffron	*saffron*
¼ pt (150 ml) dry white wine	*generous ½ cup dry white wine*
about 1¼ pt (650 ml) white stock	*3 cups white stock*
2–3 oz (50–75 g) tinned *petits pois*	*2–3 oz canned petits pois*
nut of butter	*pat of butter*
6 black olives	*6 black olives*
salt, pepper	*salt, pepper*

timbale

garnish —

Get your butcher to prepare the meat by boning and rolling it, and by cutting away the rind and most of the fat. Ask him for the bones to enrich the gravy.

Make small incisions in the meat and into these stick pieces of the sliced garlic. Put the meat in a roasting pan with the button onions and the bones, pour over half the oil and cook in a medium oven (325°F, 160°C, gas mark 3) for 1½–2 hours, or until the meat is tender. When the meat becomes golden add a little water to keep the joint moist, and some coarse salt. Turn from time to time.

While the meat is cooking sautez the rice in the rest of the oil until it is glistening (but not for more than 3 minutes). Add the chopped ham, the very finely chopped onion, one of the tomatoes, skinned and de-pipped (*seeded*), the tomato purée (*paste*), a little saffron (how much will depend on your own taste), the wine and finally the hot stock. Season, cover the pan and cook gently, stirring from time to time. About halfway through the cooking add the *petits pois*. Butter some ramekins, and when the rice is nearly dry fill them with the mixture, pressing it down well. Keep the moulds warm, loosely covered with foil, in a *bain-marie*.

Cut the remaining 2 tomatoes into slices and lay them in a small ovenproof dish with a nut (*pat*) of butter. Put them in the oven for a few minutes.

When the pork is done, transfer it to a large serving dish. Unmould the rice 'puddings', and arrange them round the meat. Place a slice of the cooked tomatoes on each, and on top of this a stoned olive. Keep warm while you make the gravy from the cooking liquor, strained and with the excess fat skimmed off. It should be served separately.

Carré de Porc–Pommes 'en l'Air'   Serves 8
(Loin of Pork with Apples)

The name of this dish, which was devised by Patrice Lelaurain's father, is a charming pun: *pomme de terre* being a potato, *pomme 'en l'air'* is obviously an apple!

4½ lb (2 kg) loin of pork	*4½ lb loin of pork*
4–5 tbs oil	*5–6 tbs oil*
about 4 oz (100 g) butter	*generous ½ cup (1 stick) butter*
1 onion	*1 onion*
3 cloves garlic	*3 cloves garlic*
a few sprigs of thyme and sage	*a few sprigs of thyme and sage*
1 bayleaf	*1 bayleaf*
½ pt (300 ml) dry white wine	*1¼ cups dry white wine*
8 dessert apples	*8 firm baking apples*
small bunch of watercress	*small bunch of watercress*
salt, pepper	*salt, pepper*

Get your butcher to prepare the meat by boning and rolling it and by cutting away the rind and most of the fat. Ask him for the bones to enrich the gravy.

Season the joint, put it in a baking tin with the bones round it, pour the oil over the top and roast in a medium oven (350°F, 180°C, gas mark 4) for about 2 hours, basting from time to time. About two-thirds of the way through skim off the fat and remove the bones. Add a nut (*pat*) of butter and the thickly sliced onion, the whole garlic cloves and the thyme, sage and bayleaf. Allow to colour slightly and add two-thirds of the wine.

Meanwhile remove the cores of the apples (but do not peel them), and put a generous knob of butter into each hole. Place the apples in an ovenproof dish with the rest of the wine, and bake in a hot oven (450°F, 230°C, gas mark 8) for 20–30 minutes, depending on the size and type of the apples. If you haven't a double oven, and the apples are cooked in the same oven as the pork, they will of course take longer.

When the pork is ready put it in the middle of a big serving dish. Arrange the apples round it, with a sprig or two of watercress in each cavity. Keep warm. Strain the liquid in which the pork was cooked, skim off any excess fat and serve separately.

Jambon Braisé au Champagne
(Ham Braised in Champagne)

a ham weighing about 4½ lb
(2 kg)
1 bottle non-vintage
champagne
bouquet garni
½ oz (12 g) cornflour
½ pt (300 ml) double or
whipping cream or *crème
fraîche*
2 oz (50 g) butter

*a ham weighing about 4½ lb
1 bottle non-vintage champagne
bouquet garni
1 tbs cornstarch
1¼ cups heavy cream or crème
fraîche
4 tbs (½ stick) butter*

Soak the ham in cold water overnight. Drain, cover with cold water and simmer very gently at a temperature of about 180°F (90°C), covered, for about 1¼ hours (15 minutes per 1 lb or ½ kg).

Lift out of the pan and remove the skin and a little of the fat. Put in a braising pan or ovenproof casserole with the champagne and the bouquet garni. Cover, and bake in a moderately hot oven (400°F, 200°C, gas mark 6) for ½–¾ hours, until quite cooked. Baste from time to time. Remove to a serving dish and keep warm.

Skim off any excess fat from the cooking liquid and reduce until the sauce has a syrupy consistency. Mix the cornflour (*cornstarch*) with a tablespoonful or two of water and stir in. Add the cream and reduce again until the sauce reaches the desired thickness. Stir in the butter, cut into small pieces, strain, and serve separately.

Rognons de Veau au Brut Impérial
(Veal Kidneys Cooked in Champagne)

Veal kidneys are substantial fare, and you may find that 2 of them are enough for 6 people. If so, you will need to have 6 slices of bread instead of 4, and increase the number of pimentoes (*peppers*) and the quantity of stuffing accordingly.

2 veal kidneys	*2 veal kidneys*
olive oil	*olive oil*
2 tbs whisky	*2 tbs whisky*
about 4 oz (100 g) butter	*generous ½ cup (1 stick) butter*
1 shallot	*1 shallot*
4 oz (100 g) button mushrooms	*¼ lb button mushrooms*
⅓ pt (200 ml) non-vintage champagne	*1 cup non-vintage champagne*
2 tbs double or whipping cream or *crème fraîche*	*2 tbs heavy cream or crème fraîche*
pinch of curry powder	*pinch of curry powder*
4 slices of bread	*4 slices of bread*
salt, pepper	*salt, pepper*

Stuffed Pimentoes: *Stuffed Peppers:*

4 smallish pimentoes (2 red, 2 green)	*4 smallish peppers (2 red, 2 green)*
3 oz (75 g) long grain rice	*½ cup long grain rice*
1 medium onion	*1 medium onion*
1 oz (25 g) butter	*2 tbs (¼ stick) butter*
2 oz (50 g) sultanas	*2 oz sultanas (golden raisins)*
a little very strong tea	*a little very strong tea*
olive oil	*olive oil*
salt, pepper	*salt, pepper*

Start by preparing the stuffed pimentoes:

Stuffed Pimentoes (Peppers): Chop the onion very finely and sweat it gently in butter. Add the rice and a generous ¼ pt (200 ml, ¾ *cup*) water. Season, cover the pan and leave over the lowest possible heat for 15–18 minutes. Meanwhile soak the sultanas (*golden raisins*) in a very little strong tea to soften them. When the rice is cooked rinse the sultanas in cold water and add.

While the rice is cooking slice off the tops of the pimentoes (*peppers*) and carefully cut out the cores and seeds without breaking the skin. Make sure that all the seeds are discarded. Blanch for about 5 minutes and refresh in cold water. Fill with the prepared rice, place in a baking pan, pour over a little olive oil and bake in a hot oven (450F, 230C, gas mark 8) for 20–25 minutes.

If the kidneys are still encased in an envelope of fat, remove all but a very thin layer. If there is no fat round the kidneys, pour a little olive oil over them. Season and roast in a hot oven (450F, 230C, gas mark 8) for 15–20 minutes. When the kidneys are sufficiently cooked, remove from the oven and pour off the fat. *Flambez* the kidneys with whisky and keep warm.

Put a nut (*pat*) of butter in the pan and gently sweat the shallot, very finely chopped, and the mushrooms, cut in four. Do not allow the shallot to colour. Add the champagne and reduce by half. Stir in the cream and the curry powder. Reduce again by a third and whisk in a little butter to make the sauce perfectly smooth. Check the seasoning.

Brown the slices of bread in a little butter and put them on a serving dish. Slice the kidneys very thinly and arrange them on top. Pour the sauce over the kidneys. Arrange the stuffed pimentoes (*peppers*) round the edge of the dish, alternating the colours.

Croûte aux Rognons
(Kidneys on Toast)

A simpler version of the preceding dish.

1½ lb (675 g) veal or lamb's
    kidneys
4 thick slices of white bread
4 oz (100 g) butter
1–2 shallots
3 tbs cognac
¼ pt (150 ml) dry white wine
1 tbs double cream or *crème*
    fraîche
salt, pepper
parsley, chervil or tarragon to
    garnish

1½ lb veal or lamb's kidneys
4 thick slices of white bread
generous ½ cup (1 stick) butter
1–2 shallots
4 tbs cognac
generous ½ cup dry white wine
1 tbs heavy cream or crème fraîche
salt, pepper
parsley, chervil or tarragon to
    garnish

Cut the crusts off the bread and fry the slices in half the butter until crisp and golden on both sides. Remove to a serving dish and keep warm.

Finely chop the kidneys and sautez briefly in the same pan over a fierce heat, seasoning at the end of the cooking time. Remove from the pan and keep warm.

Pour off the fat and replace with half the remaining butter. Finely chop the shallots and fry gently until soft. Add the cognac and *flambez*. Deglaze the pan with the wine and reduce to a few tablespoonsful. Beat in the rest of the butter. Tip the kidneys back into the sauce and add the cream. Continue to cook very gently for a few minutes without allowing the sauce to boil.

Divide between the slices of bread, sprinkle with the chopped parsley, chervil or tarragon and serve very hot.

Compared with other parts of France, Champagne has few specifically regional dishes. One of them, as the name implies, is *Potée Champenoise*. Basically a regional variation of *Pot-au-feu*, and traditionally eaten at the time of the vintage, it is a robust and filling dish – not the kind of fare that would normally be served at Saran. However, the Moët chefs will sometimes present it for a special occasion – if, for instance, visitors are invited to lunch or dinner in the Caveau Napoléon, a small area of the immense cellars beneath the *Maison* in the Avenue de Champagne which is reserved for entertaining.

The ways of making it are endless, and every chef and housewife has his or her own method, which is stoutly defended against all comers. In *Champagne: The Wine, the Land and the People* Patrick Forbes gives a splendid description of one memorable gastronomic experience when he was entertained to a *potée* created (and that is literally the word) by the wife of the keeper of Moët & Chandon's *vendangeoir*, or press-house, at Verzenay. As she explained, the beef and chicken are not quite *de rigueur* (many cooks would claim that only pork should be used), but she added them, as do other cooks, because she felt that they make the *potée* pleasanter to the taste.

1 lb (450 g) salted breast of pork	*1 lb lean bacon in one piece*
1½ lb (675 g) salted shoulder of pork	*1½ lb salted shoulder of pork*
1 lb (450 g) shin of beef in one piece	*1 lb shin of beef in one piece*
1 lb (450 g) forequarter flank or silverside of beef in one piece	*1 lb forequarter flank of beef in one piece*
1 lb (450 g) spicy continental sausage	*1 lb spicy sausage*
½ boiling fowl, jointed	*½ boiling fowl, jointed*
2 lb (1 kg) savoy cabbage	*2 lb savoy cabbage*
1 lb (450 g) carrots	*1 lb carrots*
1 lb (450 g) turnips	*1 lb turnips*
2 lb (1 kg) leeks	*2 lb leeks*
1 lb (450 g) potatoes	*1 lb potatoes*
coarse salt, pepper	*coarse salt, pepper*

Soak the salted pork in cold water for 3–4 hours, changing the water frequently to get rid of any excess saltiness. Blanch the cabbage and refresh in cold water.

Drain the pork and put all the meat except the chicken joints and sausage in a large pot, cover with hot water, bring to the boil over a moderate heat and skim (the skimming process may take anything up to 30 minutes). Simmer slowly for 1 hour covered. Add the joints of chicken, the carrots (cut in two lengthwise) the turnips, cabbage and leeks. Season. Simmer for another hour, add the sausage and the potatoes and continue to simmer. After about ½ hour remove the flank of beef, which can be eaten cold later.

When the meat and vegetables are quite cooked (3 hours should be enough for the total cooking time), strain them separately and keep warm while you serve the first course, which consists of the stock in which the *potée* has been simmering. This should be poured over thinly sliced bread in a soup tureen. It is, as Patrick Forbes says, a trifle thin and fatty, but bursting with goodness.

Carve the meat – you will need a very sharp knife for this, as the meat will be so tender that it will easily fall apart. Put the vegetables round the edge of a big serving dish and arrange the meat attractively in the centre so that the whole is as pleasing to the eye as to the palate.

The cold flank of beef, which is delicious, can be used in various ways: in shepherd's pie, for instance, or in *boeuf en miroton* (slices of meat alternating with thinly sliced onions previously cooked in a little butter, covered with diced cooked potatoes and gently warmed in the oven).

Les caves

Poulet Crécy au Brut Impérial	(Chicken Cooked in Champagne with Carrots)
Poulet Etuvé au Champagne	(Chicken Cooked in Champagne)
Poulet Sauté au Bouzy	(Chicken Cooked in Bouzy)
Volaille de Bresse dans sa Croûte au Sel en sa Compagnie Périgourdine	
Poularde Truffée aux Herbes Fraîches	(Chicken Stuffed with Fresh Herbs)
Poularde Pochée à la Crème de Ciboulette	(Poached Chicken with Chives)
Caneton Braisé 'Jubilé'	(Braised 'Jubilee' Duck)
Caneton au Poivre Vert	(Duck with Green Peppercorns)
Pintadeau à la Bacchus	(Guinea-Fowl with Grapes)
Pintadeau au Citron	(Guinea-Fowl with Lemon)
Chartreuse de Perdreau au Chou Blanc	(Chartreuse of Partridge)
Faisan Champenoise	(Pheasant Champenoise)
Salmis de Faisan	(Salmis of Pheasant)
Fricassée de Lapereau à la Moutarde de Meaux	(Rabbit Fricassee with Meaux Mustard)
Gigue de Chevreuil Sauce Poivrade	(Haunch of Venison with Game Sauce)
Civet de Lièvre à la Française	(Hare Cooked in Red Wine)

Poulet Crécy au Brut Impérial
(Chicken Cooked in Champagne with Carrots)

1 chicken 4–4½ lb (2 kg)
1–2 tbs oil
5 oz (125 g) butter
3 shallots
10 medium carrots
¼ bottle non-vintage champagne
¼ pt (150 ml) double or whipping cream or *crème fraîche*
salt, pepper, sugar

1 chicken 4–4½ lb
1–2 tbs oil
¾ cup (1¼ sticks) butter
3 shallots
10 medium carrots
¼ bottle non-vintage champagne
generous ½ cup heavy cream or crème fraîche
salt, pepper, sugar

Joint the chicken and seal (*cut up and sear*), without colouring it, in a fireproof casserole in the oil and a little of the butter. Pour off the fat and add the shallots and 3 of the carrots, very finely chopped. Add the champagne and season. Cover and simmer very gently until the chicken is cooked (about 30 minutes).

Meanwhile cut the remaining carrots in four lengthwise and slice them finely. Cook them in another pan, closely covered, with salt and pepper, a pinch or two of sugar and just enough water to prevent them from sticking.

When the chicken is tender remove from the pan, arrange on a serving dish and keep warm. Strain the cooking liquid, return to the pan, and reduce by half, add the cream and reduce again by a third.

Drain the carrots, return them to the pan with the rest of the butter and put over a high flame for a minute or two. Stir into the sauce and pour over the chicken.

Poulet Etuvé au Champagne
(Chicken Cooked in Champagne)

1 chicken 3–3½ lb (1½ kg)
2 tbs oil
2 oz (50 g) butter
12 button onions
2 tbs *marc de champagne*
2 tbs cognac
½ bottle non-vintage champagne
1 oz (25 g) flour
¼ pt (150 ml) double or
   whipping cream or *crème*
   fraîche
1 truffle (optional)
salt, pepper

1 chicken 3–3½ lb
2 tbs oil
4 tbs (½ stick) butter
12 button onions (small white)
2 tbs marc de champagne or
   Calvados
2 tbs cognac
½ bottle non-vintage champagne
2 tbs flour
generous ½ cup heavy cream or
   crème fraîche
1 truffle (optional)
salt, pepper

Cut the chicken into joints (*8 pieces*) and sautez them in a fireproof casserole in the oil and half the butter until they are golden. Add the onions and turn together for a minute. Set fire to the *marc* or Calvados and the cognac, add them and douse the flame with the champagne. Season. Cover and simmer for 30 minutes or until the chicken is tender. Lift the joints out of the casserole, remove the skin and keep the joints warm.

Strain the cooking liquor and return to the casserole. Work the remaining butter and the flour into a *beurre manié* and stir into the cooking liquid over a gentle heat. When it has thickened add the cream, and the chopped truffle if you are using one. Add the chicken and simmer for a few minutes. Arrange on a dish and serve with rice.

Poulet Sauté au Bouzy
(Chicken Cooked in Bouzy)

1 chicken 3–3½ lb (1½ kg)
2–3 oz (50–75 g) butter
4 oz (100 g) carrots
4 oz (100 g) onions
½ bottle Bouzy or good red wine
14 oz (396 g) tin artichoke
   hearts
5 oz (150 g) bacon
4 oz (100 g) chipolata sausages
6 oz (150 g) button mushrooms
1 heaped tbs cornflour
a few drops *marc de champagne*
salt, pepper
croûtons to garnish

1 chicken 3–3½ lb
4–5 tbs (generous ½ stick)
   butter
¼ lb carrots
¼ lb onions
½ bottle Bouzy or good red wine
14 oz can artichoke hearts
5 oz bacon
¼ lb chipolata (small link)
   sausages
6 oz button mushrooms
1 heaped tbs cornstarch
a few drops marc de champagne or
   Calvados
salt, pepper
croûtons to garnish

Cut the chicken into joints (*8 pieces*). Sautez for 8–10 minutes in half the butter, with the chopped carrots and onions. Season, add the wine, cover and cook gently for about 30 minutes, until the chicken is tender.

While the chicken is cooking drain the artichoke hearts and cut each into four. Cut the bacon into dice and gently fry. Grill (*broil*) the sausages. Clean the mushrooms and cook gently in the remaining butter.

When the chicken is tender stir in the cornflour (*cornstarch*) mixed with a little water. Add a few drops of *marc de champagne* or Calvados, the sausages, bacon, artichokes and mushrooms, and heat together gently. Test for seasoning and serve very hot, with croûtons.

Volaille de Bresse dans sa Croûte au Sel en sa Compagnie Périgourdine

In 1979 a competition of *Amateurs Gourmands* was organised in Lyons by the Sofitel chain of hotels, with the object of discovering the best 'Sunday cook'. The palm was carried off by Monsieur Jean-Marie Dubois, Directeur des Relations Extérieures at Moët & Chandon, for the superb dish given below.

3½–4 lb (1.8 kg) chicken	*3½–4 lb chicken*
3 chicken livers	*3 chicken livers*
3 oz (75 g) butter	*scant ½ cup (¾ stick) butter*
2 lb (1 kg) flour	*2 lb flour*
2 lb (1 kg) sea salt	*2 lb sea salt*
4 truffles	*4 truffles*
4 'leaves' of pork fat back	*4 'leaves' of pork fat back*
salt, pepper	*salt, pepper*

Carefully remove the green part from the chicken livers. Season, and sautez quickly in a little butter to colour and stiffen them. Put them inside the chicken, together with a generous amount of pepper. Truss the chicken and brown it all over in the rest of the butter. Allow to cool.

Mix together the flour and the salt, with enough water to make into a dough – you will need about 1 pt (½ l, 2½ cups). Turn on to a floured board and roll out to a bare ¼″ (½ cm) thick. Place the chicken in the middle and wrap it in the pastry, folding the edges together lengthwise so that there is a neat join along the top. Press the edges together with a little water. Secure each end in a similar manner. The chicken should be hermetically sealed (this is most important). Use the rest of the dough to wrap round the truffles, having first wrapped them in the 'leaves' of pork fat back.

Put the chicken in a floured baking pan and bake in a hot oven (485°F, 250°C, gas mark 9). After ¾ hour add the truffles and cook for a further 15 minutes. At the end of the cooking time the chicken should stay in the oven for 15 minutes, with the heat turned off and the door shut.

Remove the chicken from the oven, place on a board and cut the crust horizontally all round about halfway down. It is extremely hard, so a sharp and very rigid knife is needed – you may find that a saw-edged knife does the job better. Replace the top half of the crust and put the chicken on a serving dish. Cut the top half of the crust away from the truffles, replace, and add the truffles to the dish. Bring the chicken to the table like this, and before carving remove the top crust from the bird and the truffles.

Serve with a green salad with a vinaigrette dressing. As you carve the chicken, take out the livers, cut them up and mix them quickly into the salad.

Monsieur Dubois suggests that this dish should be accompanied by a vinaigrette dressing served separately. An alternative is to make a thin sauce of chicken stock and white wine, reduced, with some whipping (*heavy*) cream or *crème fraîche* stirred into it and reduced again, and finally with a little butter beaten in.

This is a useful dish for the hostess, since it can be prepared before the guests arrive, needs the minimum of attention, and will not suffer if it has to wait in its crust for 30–40 minutes. Though admittedly rather grand and *de luxe* with its accompaniment of truffles, for more ordinary occasions these can be replaced by young vegetables in season, preferably steamed. In this case you will, of course, need less of the *croûte au sel*.

Poularde Truffée aux Herbes Fraîches
(Chicken Stuffed with Fresh Herbs)

Serves 4

(Herb mixture under the skin)

1 chicken 3–3½ lb (1½ kg)	*1 chicken 3–3½ lb*
2 tbs chopped parsley	*2 tbs chopped parsley*
2 tbs chopped chives	*2 tbs chopped chives*
2 tbs chopped tarragon	*2 tbs chopped tarragon*
2 shallots	*2 shallots*
6 oz (150 g) mushrooms	*6 oz mushrooms*
4–5 tbs (100 ml) double or whipping cream or *crème fraîche*	*5–6 tbs heavy cream or crème fraîche*
1 oz (25 g) butter	*2 tbs (¼ stick) butter*
1 tbs olive oil	*1 tbs olive oil*
3 cloves garlic	*3 cloves garlic*
bouquet garni	*bouquet garni*
½ pt (300 ml) good chicken stock	*1¼ cups good chicken stock*
salt, pepper	*salt, pepper*

Chop the parsley, the tarragon, the chives and the shallots very finely. Squeeze the mushrooms in a cloth to get rid of the moisture and chop them finely also. Mix all together and bind with the cream. Season. Spread this stuffing under the chicken skin, distributing it well over the breast.

Brown the chicken all over in the butter and olive oil. Add the garlic, the bouquet garni and the hot stock. Roast in a moderately hot oven (400°F, 200°C, gas mark 6) for about 1¼–1½ hours.

When the chicken is cooked remove from the pan, carve and arrange on a serving dish. Keep warm. Skim off any excess fat from the cooking liquid and reduce until it has a syrupy consistency. Strain, and pour over the chicken.

Poularde Pochée à la Crème de Ciboulette
(Poached Chicken with Chives)

1 chicken 4½ lb (2 kg)	*1 chicken 4½ lb*
1 pt (½ l) chicken stock	*2½ cups chicken stock*
2 oz (50 g) chives	*2 oz chives*
4 oz (100 g) butter	*generous ½ cup (1 stick) butter*
½ oz (10 g) cornflour	*1 tbs cornstarch*
½ pt (300 ml) double or whipping cream or *crème fraîche*	*1¼ cups heavy cream or crème fraîche*
salt, pepper	*salt, pepper*

Carve the breasts and the leg-joints from the chicken and poach them gently in the seasoned stock. When they are tender remove and keep warm. Strain the stock and reduce by about half, skimming off any impurities as it boils.

Chop the chives very finely and mix half of them with half the butter, softened. Make a sauce with this butter, the cornflour (*cornstarch*) and the stock. Correct the seasoning and simmer gently for 15 minutes. Add the cream and the remaining chives, and whisk in the rest of the butter until the sauce is perfectly smooth.

Divide each of the breasts and the leg-joints into two (if the chicken breasts are very thick, slice them into thinner pieces). Arrange on a dish and pour the sauce over them.

Serve with *Pommes Paillasson*: Peel 1½ lb (675 g) potatoes and cut them into 'straws' with a mandolin. Do not wash them, but season with salt and pepper. Melt a little butter and oil in a medium sized pan. Add the potatoes, pressing them together well with a palette knife. Fry them on one side until they are golden, and turn and fry on the other side (15 minutes in all). This produces a kind of potato cake which is served up on a round dish or plate.

Caneton Braisé 'Jubilé'
(Braised 'Jubilee' Duck)

At the time of the Queen's Jubilee in 1977, chefs from many parts of Europe gathered in England to prepare banquets in various towns. The first banquet was in Southend, and M. Lelaurain's father was among the chefs chosen to prepare one of the courses. This is the dish he created for the occasion.

1 duck 4–5 lb (2–2½ kg) with its giblets
1 tbs oil
nut of butter
1 onion
1 carrot
2 cloves garlic
8 oz (225 g) tomatoes
1 tbs tomato purée
½ orange
½ lemon
1 oz (25 g) sugar
3 tbs wine vinegar
½ bottle Coteaux Champenois or dry white wine
bouquet garni
1 oz (25 g) seedless raisins
1 cup very strong tea
1 oz (25 g) black olives
salt, pepper, cayenne pepper

1 duck 4–5 lb with its giblets
1 tbs oil
pat of butter
1 onion
1 carrot
2 cloves garlic
½ lb tomatoes
1 tbs tomato paste
½ orange
½ lemon
1 heaped tbs sugar
4 tbs wine vinegar
½ bottle Coteaux Champenois or dry white wine
bouquet garni
1 oz seedless raisins
1 cup very strong tea
1 oz black olives
salt, pepper, cayenne pepper

Season the duck with salt and pepper and roast in a moderately hot oven (400°F, 200°C, gas mark 6), with the chopped giblets, for 20–25 minutes, in order to get rid of some of the fat.

Meanwhile melt the oil and butter in a fireproof casserole. Add the sliced onion and carrot and the crushed garlic and allow to sweat for about 15 minutes. Add the roughly chopped tomatoes and the tomato purée (*paste*), and continue to cook.

Grate the zest of the orange and lemon and blanch. Refresh in cold water, drain and put on one side. Squeeze the juice of the fruit and reserve this also.

Prepare the *bigarade* (bitter orange sauce). Melt the sugar in a small pan until it is golden. Off the stove slowly stir in the wine vinegar, return to the heat and boil for 5 minutes. Add the orange and lemon juice. Add to the vegetables in the casserole, together with the wine and the bouquet garni. Put the duck in the casserole, cover and simmer gently for 1–1¼ hours or until it is tender.

Steep the raisins in the strong tea for 10 minutes. Blanch the olives. Drain both well and mix with the orange and lemon zest. Sprinkle with a little cayenne pepper.

When the duck is cooked remove from the casserole, carve, arrange on a serving dish and keep warm. Strain the sauce, pressing through as much of the vegetables as possible. Stir the raisins and olives into the sauce and test for seasoning. You may want to add a little sugar, but the sauce should have a sharp taste. Pour this sauce over the duck and serve with rice or noodles.

This is a useful dish for a dinner party as it can wait for half-an-hour or so. It can also be prepared beforehand, allowing the duck to cool before you carve it (which makes this tricky task considerably easier). Reheat the duck and the sauce gently before serving.

Caneton au Poivre Vert
(Duck with Green Peppercorns)

Serves 4

1 duck 4–5 lb (2–2½ kg)	*1 duck 4–5 lb*
1 wineglass white wine	*1 wineglass white wine*
¼ pt (150 ml) veal stock	*generous ½ cup veal stock*
¼ pt (150 ml) double or	*generous ½ cup heavy cream or*
whipping cream or *crème*	*crème fraîche*
fraîche	*1 tbs green peppercorns*
1 tbs green peppercorns	*4 tbs (½ stick) butter*
2 oz (50 g) butter	*salt*
salt	

Prick the skin of the duck to allow the fat to escape as it cooks, and salt lightly. Roast on a rack in a moderately hot oven (400°F, 200°C, gas mark 6) for 1¼–1½ hours, basting from time to time. By the time the cooking is finished the duck should be crisply roasted. When it is tender remove to a serving dish and keep warm.

Discard the fat from the pan and deglaze with the wine. Add the veal stock and reduce to a few tablespoonsful. Stir in the cream and the peppercorns and whisk in the butter cut in small pieces. Allow the sauce to bubble gently until it is smooth and creamy. Correct the seasoning and serve separately.

This dish is good with pilaf rice and sautéed mushrooms.

Pintadeau à la Bacchus
(Guinea-Fowl with Grapes)

Serves 6

Chanterelles, the frilly orange mushrooms which grow in woods in summer, should ideally be used for this dish. But as they cannot be bought, and are becoming increasingly difficult to find for oneself, cultivated mushrooms will probably have to be substituted. If guinea-fowl is not available, chicken can be substituted, but it will not, of course, be quite so good.

2 guinea-fowl each about 3 lb (1½ kg)	*2 guinea-hen each about 3 lb*
2 carrots	*2 carrots*
2 onions	*2 onions*
4 cloves garlic	*4 cloves garlic*
3–4 tbs olive oil	*4–5 tbs olive oil*
about 4 oz (100 g) butter	*generous ½ cup (1 stick) butter*
12 oz (350 g) grapes, preferably muscat	*¾ lb grapes, preferably muscat*
3–4 tbs *marc de champagne*	*4–5 tbs marc de champagne or Calvados*
1 large wineglass red wine	*1 large wineglass red wine*
¼ pt (150 ml) veal stock	*generous ½ cup veal stock*
½ oz (10 g) flour	*1 tbs flour*
1 lb (450 g) mushrooms	*1 lb mushrooms*
salt, pepper	*salt, pepper*

Season the guinea-fowl (*guinea-hen*), put in a roasting pan, add the chopped-up carrots and onions and the garlic cloves, and roast in a moderately hot oven (400°F, 200°C, gas mark 6), with the oil and a little of the butter, for about 1 hour, until they are tender.

Meanwhile steep the grapes, unpeeled but with the pips (*seeds*) taken out, in the *marc de champagne* or Calvados.

When the guinea-fowl are ready remove them from the pan and keep warm. Strain the cooking liquor and remove any fat. Return to the pan and deglaze with wine and stock. Reduce, and enrich with *beurre manié*, made by working together the flour and ½ oz (10 g, *1 tbs*) of the butter. Add the *marc* in which the grapes have been steeping. Cut the mushrooms in four and sautez in butter. Sweat the grapes in a little butter.

Carve the guinea-fowl and arrange on a serving dish. Scatter the grapes on top and arrange the mushrooms round the side of the dish. Pour over a little of the sauce and serve the rest separately.

Pintadeau au Citron
(Guinea-Fowl with Lemon)

Serves 8

This is an excellent dish for a dinner-party, since all the preliminary cooking can be done beforehand. As in the previous recipe, if guinea-fowl is not available, chicken can be substituted, but it will not, of course, be quite so good.

3 guinea-fowl each about 3 lb (1½ kg)	*3 guinea-hen each about 3 lb*
2 onions	*2 onions*
2 oranges	*2 oranges*
3 lemons	*3 lemons*
1 pt (½ l) chicken stock	*2½ cups chicken stock*
4 oz (100 g) butter	*generous ½ cup (1 stick) butter*
3 tbs olive oil	*3–4 tbs olive oil*
½ pt (300 ml) double or whipping cream or *crème fraîche*	*1¼ cups heavy cream or crème fraîche*
chervil or parsley, chopped	*chervil or parsley, chopped*
salt, pepper	*salt, pepper*

Mousse of Pears and Spinach: *Mousse of Pears and Spinach:*

4 large dessert pears	*4 large eating pears*
8 oz (225 g) sugar	*1¼ cups sugar*
8 tbs white wine vinegar	*10 tbs white wine vinegar*
5 lb (2¼ kg) spinach	*5 lb spinach*
6 tbs double or whipping cream or *crème fraîche*	*7–8 tbs heavy cream or crème fraîche*
3 oz (75 g) butter	*scant ½ cup (¾ stick) butter*
salt, pepper	*salt, pepper*

Compote of Onions and Sherry: *Compote of Onions and Sherry:*

8 medium onions	*8 medium onions*
4 oz (100 g) butter	*generous ½ cup (1 stick) butter*
8 tbs sherry	*10 tbs sherry*
salt, pepper, sugar	*salt, pepper, sugar*

Joint the guinea-fowl (*guinea-hen*). Season, and marinade for 6 hours or so with the chopped onion, the lemon and orange juice and the chicken stock.

Meanwhile prepare the two garnishes:

Mousse of Pears and Spinach: Make a very light syrup with 2 pts (1¼ l, 4½ *cups*) water, the sugar and the wine vinegar. Boil for a few minutes before adding the peeled, halved and cored pears. Cover and simmer for about 30 minutes, or until the pears are soft. Leave them to cool in the syrup. Trim the spinach and blanch in plenty of boiling water, refresh in cold water and strain, pressing out all the water. Drain the pears and liquidise with the spinach to a purée. Return to the pan and leave over a low heat to extract all the liquid. Stir in the cream and the butter, season, and keep warm.

Compote of Onions and Sherry: Slice the onions thinly and sweat them in the butter, with salt and pepper and a little sugar, until they are lightly coloured and quite soft. Add the sherry. Put in an ovenproof dish, cover with foil and finish the cooking in a moderately hot oven (400F, 200C, gas mark 6) for about 20 minutes. At the end of this time the onions should have absorbed the sherry, but keep an eye on them to make sure that they don't become dry.

Take the pieces of guinea-fowl (*guinea-hen*) out of the marinade and dry them well. In about half the butter and all the oil, brown them in a sauté pan or frying pan, and put them in a moderately hot oven for about 30 minutes (400F, 200C, gas mark 6) to finish the cooking.

Sweat the marinading onion in the rest of the butter for a few minutes, then add the marinading liquid and boil hard to reduce, strain, add the cream and reheat, stirring in a little chopped chervil or parsley.

Arrange the guinea-fowl on a serving dish and pour the sauce over the top. Serve the two garnishes in separate vegetable dishes.

Chartreuse de Perdreau au Chou Blanc
(Chartreuse of Partridge)

*cooke
ou d art
chick
mea*

4 partridges or 2 pheasants	*4 partridges or 2 pheasants*
2 turnips	*2 turnips*
5 large carrots	*5 large carrots*
2 medium white cabbages	*2 medium white cabbages*
1 tbs wine vinegar	*1 tbs wine vinegar*
3 onions	*3 onions*
1 clove	*1 clove*
1 bayleaf	*1 bayleaf*
1 or 2 sprigs thyme	*1 or 2 sprigs thyme*
9 rashers smoked streaky bacon	*9 slices bacon*
6 peppercorns	*6 peppercorns*
8 oz (225 g) garlic sausage	*½ lb garlic sausage*
1 tbs butter	*1 tbs butter*
1 tbs oil	*1 tbs oil*
3 shallots	*3 shallots*
2 tbs tomato purée	*2 tbs tomato paste*
½ pt (300 ml) non-vintage champagne or dry white wine	*1¼ cups non-vintage champagne or dry white wine*
¼ pt (150 ml) chicken stock	*generous ½ cup chicken stock*
bouquet garni	*bouquet garni*
2 cloves garlic	*2 cloves garlic*
salt, pepper	*salt, pepper*
1 tbs chopped parsley to garnish	*1 tbs chopped parsley to garnish*

Peel the turnips and 2 of the carrots and boil them whole. Drain and reserve. As these vegetables will be used mainly for decoration, their appearance can be enhanced by cannelling them before you cook them.

Soak the cabbages in water, with the vinegar, to clean them. Drain and cut each one into four. Put them in a large pan with 1 of the onions stuck with the clove, the bayleaf, thyme, 4 rashers (*slices*) of bacon, 1 carrot and the peppercorns. Add salted water just to cover. Put a closely fitting lid on the pan and cook slowly for 2 hours. Add the garlic sausage for the last 20 minutes. At the end of the cooking time remove the garlic sausage and drain off the cabbage, pressing well to remove all the water. Reserve both.

While the cabbages are cooking, cut the partridges in half or the pheasants in four and season. In a large pan melt the butter and oil. Sweat the rest of the bacon in this, then add the pieces of bird and sautez for a few minutes until they are a nice brown. Remove the birds and cut the meat neatly from the bones. Remove the bacon and put on one side.

Chop the remaining onions, 2 of the shallots and the 2 remaining carrots, and brown them in the fat left in the pan. Pour off any excess fat. Add the tomato purée (*paste*) and return the bacon and pieces of bird. Add the champagne or white wine, reduce slightly and moisten with the chicken stock. Add the bouquet garni and the garlic cloves, cover, and cook over a low heat for ½ hour. Remove the pieces of bird.

Well butter two 7″ (12 cm) charlotte moulds or soufflé dishes. Slice the garlic sausage and the 2 turnips and carrots which you cooked first into neat, thin rounds and line the bottoms of the moulds with half of them, alternating the colours and overlapping the rounds. On this put a layer of half the cabbage, then a layer of bacon, a layer of partridge meat and a second layer of cabbage. Finish with another neat layer of turnips, carrots and garlic sausage.

Strain the cooking liquid from the pan in which the birds were cooked and pour about half into the moulds, keeping the rest warm. Cover the moulds, and cook in a *bain-marie* in a moderate oven (350°F, 180°C, gas mark 4) for about 30 minutes, or until the *chartreuse* has heated through. Turn out on to serving dishes and strain off any juice. Pour over a little of the sauce which you have been keeping warm and serve the rest separately. Sprinkle parsley over the *chartreuse* before serving.

Faisan Champenoise
(Pheasant Champenoise)

1 pheasant with its giblets
2 oz (50 g) pork fat
2 shallots
½ tin ceps or 4 oz (100 g)
   mushrooms
4 oz (100 g) breadcrumbs
1 egg-yolk and 1 whole egg
fines herbes
1 slice cooked ham
about 4 oz (100 g) butter
30 large white grapes
3 tbs cognac
flour
rind of 1 lemon
2 oz (50 g) pine kernels
   (optional)
¼ pt (150 ml) non-vintage
   champagne
¼ pt (150 ml) double or
   whipping cream or *crème
   fraîche*
clarified butter for frying
salt, pepper

1 pheasant with its giblets
2 oz pork fat
2 shallots
½ can ceps or ¼ lb mushrooms
2½ cups breadcrumbs
1 egg-yolk and 1 whole egg
fines herbes
1 slice cooked ham
generous ½ cup (1 stick) butter
30 large white grapes
4 tbs cognac
flour
rind of 1 lemon
2 oz pine nuts (optional)
*generous ½ cup non-vintage
   champagne*
*generous ½ cup heavy cream or
   crème fraîche*
clarified butter for frying
salt, pepper

Cut up the pheasant's liver and toss in the pork fat with the chopped shallots and the chopped ceps or mushrooms. Off the fire, stir in three-quarters of the breadcrumbs, the egg-yolk and some *fines herbes*, chopped. Mix well together and season.

Remove the wing bones from the pheasant. Fill it with the stuffing and season it. Tie securely so that the stuffing does not ooze out. Cover the breast with the slice of ham (if you have a vine-leaf to hand put this on the breast first!) and cook in a well-buttered casserole with about half the butter, covered, in a moderately hot oven (400°F, 200°C, gas mark 6) for about 1 hour, until the bird is tender, basting from time to time. Remove the ham for the last 10–15 minutes so that the breast can brown. Take out the pheasant, put on a serving dish and keep warm.

Meanwhile, de-pip (*seed*) – but do not peel – the grapes and steep for 10 minutes in the cognac. Drain, and roll first in half the remaining butter, melted, then in the flour, next in the whole egg beaten, and finally in the remaining breadcrumbs. This is quickly done by putting each of these ingredients in a separate soup plate and rolling the grapes all together successively in each one. Slice the lemon peel *julienne* and blanch it for 5 minutes with the pine kernels (*nuts*), if you are using them.

Gently sweat the wings and neck of the pheasant in the casserole in which the bird was cooked. Deglaze with the champagne. Remove the wings and neck, add the cream and reduce by about a third. Enrich this sauce with the rest of the butter and add the lemon peel and the pine kernels.

At the last moment, quickly fry the grapes in the clarified butter. (It is important that it should be clarified, or else they will burn.)

Serve the pheasant surrounded by the grapes and the sauce separately in a sauce-boat.

Salmis de Faisan
(Salmis of Pheasant)

1 pheasant (a cock bird is best) with its liver	*1 pheasant (a cock bird is best) with its liver*
4 oz (100 g) butter	*generous ½ cup (1 stick) butter*
1 onion	*1 onion*
1 carrot	*1 carrot*
3 cloves garlic	*3 cloves garlic*
20 juniper berries	*20 juniper berries*
bouquet garni	*bouquet garni*
⅓ pt (200 ml) Madeira	*1 cup Madeira*
4 tbs cognac	*5 tbs cognac*
½ pt (300 ml) non-vintage champagne or dry white wine	*1¼ cups non-vintage champagne or dry white wine*
salt, pepper	*salt, pepper*

Season the pheasant, spread about a third of the butter over its breast, and roast until half-cooked (about 30 minutes in a medium oven (350°F, 180°C, gas mark 4)). Remove from the roasting pan and allow to cool.

While the pheasant is cooking chop the onion, carrot and garlic finely and sweat them in the rest of the butter in a fireproof casserole over a low heat.

When the pheasant is cold carve it and lay the pieces in another casserole, well buttered. Add the crushed juniper berries and the bouquet garni, and sprinkle with a little of the Madeira and a little of the cognac. Cover tightly and put in a cool oven (250°F, 120°C, gas mark ½) to cook very slowly for 1 hour.

Meanwhile crush the pheasant carcass and add it to the vegetables. Pour in the rest of the Madeira and cognac and the champagne. Season. Cover and also cook slowly for 1 hour. Strain, and bind by adding the raw pheasant's liver, creamed (*mashed*). Beat this in over a low heat. Do not allow the sauce to boil.

Arrange the pieces of pheasant on a serving dish, pour the sauce over the top and serve.

Fricassée de Lapereau à la Moutarde de Meaux
(Rabbit Fricassee with Meaux Mustard)

Serves 4

1 young rabbit about 3 lb (1½ kg)	*1 young rabbit about 3 lb*
3 tbs oil	*3 tbs oil*
4 oz (100 g) butter	*generous ½ cup (1 stick) butter*
3 shallots	*3 shallots*
2 cloves garlic	*2 cloves garlic*
1 lb (450 g) mushrooms	*1 lb mushrooms*
1 pt (½ l) dry white wine	*2½ cups dry white wine*
bouquet garni	*bouquet garni*
½ pt (300 ml) double or whipping cream or *crème fraîche*	*1¼ cups heavy cream or crème fraîche*
1–2 tbs Meaux mustard	*2–3 tbs Meaux mustard*
1 lemon	*1 lemon*
salt, pepper	*salt, pepper*

Cut up the rabbit and season. Heat the oil and half the butter in a sauté pan and colour the pieces. Add the shallots, the garlic cloves and a dozen mushroom stalks, all finely chopped. Pour in the wine and add the bouquet garni. Season. Cover the pan and leave to cook gently for about 30 minutes.

When the rabbit is tender remove to a serving dish and keep warm. Strain the sauce and reduce to about ¾ pt (425 ml, 1¾ *cups*). Add the cream and reduce again by about half. Add the mustard to the sauce – but do not allow to boil – and keep warm in a *bain-marie*.

Chop the mushrooms and put them in another pan with the rest of the butter, salt and the juice of the lemon. Cook rapidly until the liquid has nearly evaporated. Spoon over the rabbit and pour the sauce over the top.

Gigue de Chevreuil Sauce Poivrade
(Haunch of Venison with Game Sauce)

6 lb (2½ kg) haunch of venison
   with bones and trimmings
larding bacon or pork fat back
4 tbs truffle juice and 4 tbs
   cognac *or* 6 tbs cognac
2 tbs oil
2 onions
2 shallots
1 large carrot
1 tbs tomato purée
4 tbs wine vinegar
1 pt (½ l) red wine
beef consommé or veal stock
bouquet garni
about 3 oz (75 g) butter
salt, pepper

6 lb haunch of venison with bones
   and trimmings
larding bacon or pork fat back
5 tbs truffle juice and 5 tbs cognac
   or 7–8 tbs cognac
2 tbs oil
2 onions
2 shallots
1 large carrot
1 tbs tomato paste
5 tbs wine vinegar
2½ cups red wine
beef consommé or veal stock
bouquet garni
scant ½ cup (¾ stick) butter
salt, pepper

Lard or bard the venison (see p22). Alternatively, cut the bacon or pork fat back into small cubes, stiffen them in iced water, strain, and insert them into the haunch as if you were inserting cloves of garlic in a leg of lamb. Put the venison in a bowl just large enough to hold it, and pour over the truffle juice, if you are using it, and the cognac, or the larger quantity of cognac alone. Leave to marinade for 6 hours or more, turning from time to time.

Meanwhile break up the bones and put them in a casserole with the trimmings from the meat and a little oil. Brown well, then add the chopped onions, shallots and carrot. Stir in the tomato purée (*paste*). Skim off any fat and deglaze the pan with the vinegar. Simmer for several minutes to reduce. Add the wine and reduce again. Pour in enough stock to come halfway up the bones, add the bouquet garni, season, cover the pan and simmer for 1 hour, or until the liquid has reduced by about half and has the consistency of thin cream. Strain and put on one side.

When you are ready to cook the meat remove from the marinade and dry very well. Put in a very hot oven (500°F, 260°C, gas mark 9). Immediately turn down the oven to 350°F, 180°C, gas mark 4 and roast for 20 minutes per 1 lb ($\frac{1}{2}$ kg), basting frequently.

When the venison is cooked, carve it as you would a leg of mutton. Arrange on a serving dish and keep warm. Reheat the sauce and add to it the strained marinading liquid. Add the butter, cut up into small pieces, and stir until the sauce is perfectly smooth. Serve separately.

A purée of chestnuts or celeriac, and red currant, wortleberry or rowan jelly go well with this dish.

Civet de Lièvre à la Française
(Hare Cooked in Red Wine)

1 hare
1 oz (25 g) flour
butter ⎱ for frying
oil ⎰
5 oz (150 g) thick-cut streaky
    bacon
2 carrots
1 onion
3 cloves garlic
bouquet garni
1 bayleaf
6 oz (150 g) mushrooms
4 tbs cognac
1 bottle Bouzy or good red wine
20 button onions
about 3 oz (75 g) butter
1 teasp sugar
1 pt (½ l) hare's blood or veal or
    pork blood
½ pt (300 ml) semi-sour cream
    (2–3 tbs sour cream stirred
    into fresh double cream)
¼ pt (150 ml) fresh double
    cream or *crème fraîche*
salt, pepper

Marinade:

1 bottle red wine
2 carrots
1 onion
2 sprigs thyme
1 bayleaf
a few sprigs parsley
30 peppercorns
1 tbs olive oil

croûtons ⎱ to garnish
parsley ⎰

1 hare
2 tbs flour
butter ⎱ *for frying*
oil ⎰
5 oz thick-cut bacon
2 carrots
1 onion
3 cloves garlic
bouquet garni
1 bayleaf
6 oz mushrooms
5 tbs cognac
1 bottle Bouzy or good red wine
20 button onions (small white)
scant ½ cup (¾ stick) butter
1 teasp sugar
2½ cups hare's blood or veal or pork
    blood
1¼ cups semi-sour cream (2–3 tbs
    sour cream stirred into fresh
    heavy cream)
generous ½ cup fresh heavy cream
    or crème fraîche
salt, pepper

Marinade:

1 bottle red wine
2 carrots
1 onion
2 sprigs thyme
1 bayleaf
a few sprigs parsley
30 peppercorns
1 tbs olive oil

croûtons ⎱ *to garnish*
parsley ⎰

Cut up the hare and put to marinade in the red wine with the chopped carrots and onion, the thyme, bayleaf, parsley, peppercorns and olive oil. Leave for a minimum of 12 hours, turning from time to time.

Remove all the pieces of hare and dry well. Coat thinly with some of the flour and season. Brown all over in a mixture of butter and oil. Dice the bacon, blanch and drain. Melt in a large casserole, remove and reserve. Sweat the chopped carrots and onion and the unpeeled garlic in the bacon fat. Add the pieces of hare, the bouquet garni, the bayleaf and the chopped mushroom stalks (keeping the caps for garnish). *Flambez* the cognac and add. Sprinkle with the remaining flour and place the casserole in a hot oven for 5 minutes. Take out, pour off any excess fat and add the Bouzy or red wine. Cover, and cook in a moderate oven (350°F, 180°C, gas mark 4) for at least 2 hours, depending on the age and tenderness of the hare.

While the hare is cooking blanch the button (*small white*) onions and cook them in a small pan for 20 minutes with about half the butter and the sugar.

Remove the pieces of hare to a serving dish and keep warm. Mix the blood with the semi-sour cream and pour into the casserole. Boil for 2 minutes. Adjust the seasoning. Enrich the sauce with the fresh cream and with a nut (*pat*) of butter and keep warm while you quickly sautez the mushroom caps in the remaining butter.

Strain the sauce over the hare and garnish the dish with the mushroom caps, the button onions, the diced bacon and some croûtons. Sprinkle chopped parsley over the top and serve very hot.

l'Orangerie du Jardin Français

Desserts

Poires Almina	(Bavarois with Pears)
Sabayon	
Gratin de Fruits Rouges au Champagne or *Fraises Eugénie*	(Red Fruits with Sabayon)
Profiteroles aux Fraises	(Profiteroles with Strawberries)
Marquise Alice	(Bavarois with Praline)
Pudding Malakoff	(Bavarois with Almonds and Raisins)
Biscuit Glacé à l'Orange	(Orange Ice Cream)
Crème Favorite	
Sorbet au Marc de Champagne	
Soufflé Glacé au Café	(Iced Coffee Soufflé)
Soufflé Glacé au Citron	(Iced Lemon Soufflé)
Pots de Crème à l'Orange	
Soufflé Glacé aux Noisettes	(Iced Hazelnut Soufflé)
Vacherin à l'Abricot	(Apricot Vacherin)
Nougatine Glacée	(Praline Ice Cream)
Gâteau 'Marronnier'	(Chestnut Pudding)
Tarte aux Raisins	(Grape Tart)
Gâteau au Fromage Blanc	(Cheese Tart)
Fraises Opéra	
Bananes en Papillotes	

Poires Almina
(Bavarois with Pears)

Pears:
6 pears (Comice if possible)
3 oz (75 g) sugar
vanilla pod

Bavarois:
6 oz (150 g) sugar
4 egg-yolks
¾ pt (425 ml) milk
vanilla pod
½ oz (12 g) gelatine
½ pt (300 ml) double cream

Garnish:
1 orange
4–5 tbs (100 ml) cointreau
½ pt (300 ml) double cream

Pears:
6 pears (Comice if possible)
scant ½ cup sugar
vanilla bean

Bavarois:
scant 1 cup sugar
4 egg-yolks
1¾ cups milk
vanilla bean
3 level teasp gelatine
1¼ cups whipping cream

Garnish:
1 orange
5–6 tbs cointreau
1¼ cups whipping cream

Pears: Peel the pears, keeping the stalks on, and gently poach them for 20 minutes, or until they are soft, in a syrup made from ½ pt (300 ml, 1¼ cups) water, the sugar and the vanilla pod (*bean*). Remove the vanilla pod and leave the pears to cool in the cooking liquid.

Bavarois: Beat the sugar with the egg-yolks. Bring the milk to the boil with the vanilla pod (*bean*), remove the vanilla pod and stir the milk into the egg mixture. Return to the pan and stir over a low heat with a wooden spoon until the custard just coats the spoon. Melt the gelatine in 2 tbs water and stand in a pan of hot water to dissolve completely. Slowly stir this into the custard, strain, and allow to cool. Whip the cream lightly and fold into the custard. Pour into an oiled mould and place in the refrigerator for 2–3 hours until it is firm.

Garnish: Thinly peel the zest of the orange and cut it into *julienne* strips. Blanch for 5–6 minutes and drain. Macerate in the cointreau. Whip the cream lightly, and add the strained cointreau from the marinade.

To assemble: Turn the bavarois on to a serving dish. Drain the pears well and arrange them round it, stalks uppermost. Decorate with the whipped cream and the orange zest.

Sabayon

This is, of course, the French version of *zabaglione*, but made at Saran – to its great advantage – with champagne instead of marsala. It is sometimes, like *zabaglione*, served on its own, in glasses, but is more often served as a sauce, as with *Pudding Malakoff* (see p142).

6 egg-yolks	*6 egg-yolks*
7 oz (200 g) caster sugar	*generous 1 cup superfine sugar*
¼ bottle non-vintage champagne	*¼ bottle non-vintage champagne*

Whisk the egg-yolks and sugar together to the consistency of thick cream. Place the bowl over a pan of simmering water, whisking vigorously while gradually adding the champagne. Go on whisking until the mixture doubles in bulk and is thick and fluffy. Remove from heat and for preference serve immediately. However, if the hostess is also the chef this can be difficult, and in fact the sabayon will keep perfectly well for several hours, or even overnight in the refrigerator. It won't be warm, but will be light and delicious none the less.

It is a great boon to be able to prepare it beforehand, especially if it is to be used as a sauce. If it is not to be eaten at once, when you remove it from the heat go on beating until it is cold. Then leave in the refrigerator until you need it.

Gratin de Fruits Rouges au Champagne   *Serves 6*
or *Fraises Eugénie*
(Red Fruits with Sabayon)

This delicious dessert can be made with strawberries alone, or with peaches gently poached in a little syrup (in which case it appears on the menu as *Pêches Eugénie*).

1 lb (450 g) strawberries *or* 8 oz (225 g) strawberries and 8 oz (225 g) *fraises des bois*
8 oz (225 g) raspberries
4 oz (100 g) red currants
8 oz (225 g) caster sugar
2–3 tbs mandarine liqueur or curaçao
3 egg-yolks
¼ pt (150 ml) non-vintage champagne
¼ pt (150 ml) double or whipping cream or *crème fraîche*
icing sugar

1 pint strawberries or ½ pint strawberries and ½ pint fraises des bois
½ pint raspberries
¼ pint red currants
½ lb (1⅓ cups) superfine sugar
2−3 tbs mandarine liqueur or curaçao
3 egg-yolks
generous ½ cup non-vintage champagne
generous ½ cup whipping cream or crème fraîche
confectioners' sugar

Wash and dry the fruit and sprinkle it with half the caster (*superfine*) sugar and the mandarine liqueur or curaçao. Leave for an hour or so.

When you are ready to serve this dessert, transfer the fruit to a shallow heatproof dish. Lightly beat the cream. Make the sabayon with the egg-yolks, the remaining caster sugar and the champagne (see p138). Fold in the whipped cream and spread over the fruit. Sprinkle generously with icing (*confectioners'*) sugar and put under a medium hot grill or salamander until the 'topping' of sabayon is golden. Watch carefully to see that it does not burn. Serve at once.

Profiteroles aux Fraises
(Profiteroles with Strawberries)

2 lb (1 kg) strawberries	*2 pints strawberries*
Choux Pastry:	*Choux Pastry:*
3½ oz (90 g) flour	*scant 1 cup flour*
scant ⅓ pt (185 ml) water	*1 cup water*
3 oz (75 g) butter	*scant ½ cup (¾ stick) butter*
½ level teasp salt	*½ level teasp salt*
3–4 eggs	*3–4 eggs*
½ pt (300 ml) *crème chantilly* (see p23)	*1¼ cups crème chantilly (see p23)*
icing sugar	*confectioners' sugar*
sabayon sauce (see p138)	*sabayon sauce (see p138)*

Choux pastry: Sift the flour on to a piece of greaseproof paper. Boil the water with the butter and salt, remove from the heat and add all the flour at once, stirring vigorously until the mixture is smooth. Return to a low heat and beat for a minute to dry out the mixture. Cool, and beat in the eggs one by one until the dough is smooth and shiny. Do not add the whole of the fourth egg if it will make the dough too sloppy to handle easily, and in any case reserve a little of it for brushing the pastry. Pipe the dough in little balls on to a buttered baking sheet about 2″ (5 cm) apart. Brush with the beaten egg and bake in a moderately hot oven (400°F, 200°C, gas mark 6) for 15–20 minutes or until firm and golden brown. Cool on a rack, splitting the puffs while still hot to release the steam.

To assemble: When the puffs are cold (but not more than 2 hours before serving) fill them with the *crème chantilly* and arrange on a large serving dish. Hull and clean the strawberries and alternate them with the profiteroles. Sprinkle the strawberries with icing (*confectioners'*) sugar.

Serve the sabayon sauce separately. If possible this should be made just before it is to be eaten, so that it is still warm, but if this is too difficult for the hostess-cook it can be prepared beforehand and served cold (it will still be excellent).

Marquise Alice
(Bavarois with Praline)

½ pt (300 ml) milk
vanilla pod
3 egg-yolks
3 oz (75 g) caster sugar
2 teasps gelatine
⅓ pt (200 ml) double cream
3 oz (75 g) praline (see p27)
about 20 'Boudoir' sponge
    fingers
4–5 tbs anisette or Grand
    Marnier
¼ pt (150 ml) *crème chantilly* (see
    p23)
red currant jelly

1¼ cups milk
vanilla bean
3 egg-yolks
½ cup superfine sugar
2 teasps gelatine
1 cup whipping cream
¾ cup praline (see p27)
about 6 oz ladyfingers
5–6 tbs anisette or Grand
    Marnier
generous ½ cup crème chantilly (see
    p23)
red currant jelly

Scald the vanilla pod (*bean*) in the milk, bringing it slowly to the boil. Beat the egg-yolks and sugar vigorously together. Remove the vanilla pod and pour the milk on to the egg-yolks and sugar, stirring as you do so. Return to the pan and stir constantly over a low heat with a wooden spoon. Test when the custard is ready by passing your finger over the back of the spoon: this will leave a streak, and the custard should not run back for a few seconds. Do not allow the custard to boil.

In a small bowl melt the gelatine in a tablespoon of cold water. Stand the bowl in a pan of hot water until the gelatine has completely dissolved. Stir into the custard and leave to cool. Beat the cream lightly and fold it in. Put into the refrigerator or freeze until it is just starting to set. Fold in the praline.

Lightly oil a 2¼ pt (1½ l, 5½ *cup*) charlotte mould. Dip the sponge fingers (*ladyfingers*) into the anisette or Grand Marnier and line the sides and bottom of the mould. Pour in the *bavarois* and refrigerate for at least 4 hours, or until it sets. When you are ready to serve it, turn out and cover with *crème chantilly*. Surround with a ring of barely melted red currant jelly.

Pudding Malakoff
Serves 8

(Bavarois with Almonds and Raisins)

A very prosaic name for a mouth-watering and most unpudding-like dessert.

grated zest of 2 oranges	*grated zest of 2 oranges*
2 oz (50 g) seedless raisins	*½ cup seedless raisins*
1 cup strong tea	*1 cup strong tea*
½ pt (300 ml) milk	*1¼ cups milk*
vanilla pod	*vanilla bean*
3 egg-yolks	*3 egg-yolks*
3 oz (75 g) caster sugar	*½ cup superfine sugar*
2 teasps gelatine	*2 teasps gelatine*
⅓ pt (200 ml) double cream	*1 cup whipping cream*
2 oz (50 g) slivered almonds	*½ cup slivered almonds*
about 20 'Boudoir' sponge fingers	*about 6 oz ladyfingers*
4–5 tbs curaçao or Grand Marnier	*5–6 tbs curaçao or Grand Marnier*
sabayon sauce (½ the quantity given on p138)	*sabayon sauce (½ the quantity given on p138)*
1–2 tbs kirsch	*1–2 tbs kirsch*

Blanch the orange zest for a few minutes and strain. Reserve. Soak the raisins for about 15 minutes in the tea to soften and swell them. Strain, rinse in cold water and reserve.

Scald the vanilla pod (*bean*) in the milk, bringing it slowly to the boil. Beat the egg-yolks and sugar vigorously together. Remove the vanilla pod and pour the milk on to the egg-yolks and sugar, stirring as you do so. Return to the pan and stir constantly with a wooden spoon over a low heat. Test when the custard is ready by passing your finger over the back of the spoon: this will leave a streak, and the custard should not run back for a few seconds. Do not allow the custard to boil.

In a small bowl melt the gelatine in a tablespoon of cold water. Stand the bowl in a pan of hot water until the gelatine has completely dissolved. Stir into the custard and leave to cool. Beat the cream lightly and fold it in. Put in the refrigerator or freezer until the custard is just starting to set. Fold in the orange zest, the raisins and the slivered almonds.

142

Lightly oil a 2¼ pt (1½ l, 5½ *cup*) charlotte mould. Dip the sponge fingers (*ladyfingers*) into the curaçao or Grand Marnier and line the sides and bottom of the mould. Pour in the *bavarois* and refrigerate for at least 4 hours or until it sets. When you are ready to serve it, turn on to a dish. Accompany it with a sabayon sauce with a little kirsch added.

Biscuit Glacé à l'Orange   *Serves 8*
(Orange Ice Cream)

1 orange	*1 orange*
3 tbs orange curaçao or other orange-flavoured liqueur	*4 tbs orange curaçao or other orange-flavoured liqueur*
7 oz (200 g) icing sugar	*2 scant cups confectioners' sugar*
6 eggs	*6 eggs*
1 pt (½ l) single cream	*2½ cups light cream*
½ pt (300 ml) *crème chantilly* (see p23)	*1¼ cups crème chantilly (see p23)*

Grate the orange zest, blanch for a few minutes, drain and steep in the orange curaçao. Work together the sifted icing (*confectioners'*) sugar and the egg-yolks. Fold in the stiffly beaten egg-whites. Stir in the single (*light*) cream, the orange zest and the curaçao and pour into a mould. Freeze.

With a sharp pointed knife, remove the skin from the orange, cutting down to the flesh so that none of the pith remains. Carefully remove each segment of orange by cutting down to the core close to the membrane.

To serve, turn out of the mould and decorate with *crème chantilly* and the orange segments.

This delectable ice cream can be eaten straight from the freezer.

143

4 egg-whites
8 oz (225 g) caster sugar
1 pt (½ l) double cream
1–1½ lb (450–675 g) raspberries
icing sugar
kirsch or framboise

4 egg-whites
½ lb (1⅓ cups) superfine sugar
2½ cups whipping cream
1–1½ pints fresh raspberries or 2
    10 oz packets frozen
confectioners' sugar
kirsch or framboise

Make some meringues with the egg-whites and the caster (*superfine*) sugar (see p150 for method). As they will be broken into pieces, it doesn't matter what shape you make them in.

Beat the cream until it is light and fluffy and fold in the broken meringue, which should be in fairly large pieces. Put into a 3 pt (1½ l, *7 cup*) bombe mould or soufflé dish and freeze for 3–4 hours or overnight.

Liquidise the raspberries and put them through a fine sieve. Mix with icing (*confectioners'*) sugar to taste and add the kirsch or framboise – enough to give a definite flavour.

When you are ready to serve the dish, turn out the meringue mixture and cover with the raspberry purée.

Sorbet au Marc de Champagne

1 lb (450 g) sugar	*generous 2 cups sugar*
1 pt (½ l) non-vintage champagne	*2½ cups non-vintage champagne*
2 lemons	*2 lemons*
1 orange	*1 orange*
2–3 tbs *marc de champagne*	*3–4 tbs marc de champagne or Calvados*

Boil the sugar and 1¾ pt (1 l, *4 cups*) water for 15–20 minutes until they have reduced to about 1 pt (½ l, *2½ cups*) syrup. Cool. Add the champagne, the juice of the lemons and the orange and the *marc* (*or Calvados*). Put in the freezer. When the mixture starts to freeze and to become mushy beat very well and replace in the freezer. Serve straight from the freezer in pretty wineglasses.

Without a commercial *sorbetière* it is impossible to achieve the cloudlike fluffiness of the sorbets which are served at the château de Saran. But a good enough consistency can be achieved if the midway beating is vigorous enough. You may need to set your freezer lower than usual, as this sorbet has such a high sugar content.

Soufflé Glacé au Café
(Iced Coffee Soufflé)

At Saran this soufflé is made with extract of coffee, which can be bought without difficulty there. Outside France it is less easy to obtain, so if necessary substitute instant coffee.

4 whole eggs and 2 egg-whites	*4 whole eggs and 2 egg-whites*
5 oz (125 g) caster sugar	*scant 1 cup superfine sugar*
1 liqueur glass coffee extract *or*	*1 liqueur glass coffee extract or*
3 teasp instant coffee	* 3 teasp instant coffee dissolved*
dissolved in 1 tbs boiling	* in 1 tbs boiling water*
water	*1¼ cups whipping cream or crème*
½ pt (300 ml) double cream or	* fraîche*
crème fraîche	*coarse instant coffee or chocolate*
coarse instant coffee or chocolate	*'sprinklers' to garnish*
sugar strands to garnish	

Prepare a 1½ pt (1 l, 3½ *cup*) soufflé mould by tying round it a collar of greaseproof paper to come about 3″ (7 cm) above the rim. Secure tightly with string or Scotch tape.

Beat the egg-yolks and all but 1 tbs of the sugar in a bowl over gently simmering water until the mixture becomes thick and frothy (but do not leave over the water so long that it sticks to the side of the basin). Remove from the heat and beat vigorously, preferably with a powerful electric beater, until cold. Add the coffee extract. Beat the 6 egg-whites stiffly, incorporating the remaining 1 tbs sugar towards the end of the beating. Fold into the mixture a few spoonfuls at a time, and finally fold in the lightly beaten cream. Pour into the soufflé mould and freeze for about 4 hours or until the soufflé is lightly frozen. Before serving, remove the paper collar and sprinkle the top thickly with instant coffee or chocolate sugar strands ('*sprinklers*').

If you make the soufflé in advance, so that it is frozen hard, take it out of the freezer about 1 hour before you want to serve it and leave in the refrigerator.

Soufflé Glacé au Citron
(Iced Lemon Soufflé)

2 large lemons	*2 large lemons*
6 eggs	*6 eggs*
7 oz (200 g) caster sugar	*generous 1 cup superfine sugar*
¾ pt (425 ml) double cream	*1¾ cups whipping cream*

Prepare a 2 pt (1¼ l, *4½ cup*) soufflé mould by tying round it a collar of greaseproof paper to come about 3″ (7 cm) above the rim. Secure tightly with string or Scotch tape.

Grate the lemon peel and squeeze out the juice. In a bowl or the top of a double saucepan beat the egg-yolks and sugar until the mixture is smooth and fluffy. Place over a pan of barely simmering water and continue to beat until it expands and thickens slightly (but do not leave over the water so long that it sticks to the sides of the basin). Remove from the heat and beat vigorously, preferably with a powerful electric beater, until cool. Stir in the grated lemon peel and the juice, and two or three spoonfuls at a time gently fold in first the stiffly beaten egg-whites and then the lightly beaten cream. As lemons vary so much in size and the amount of juice they yield, it is advisable to taste at this stage, and add a little more lemon juice if necessary.

Pour into the soufflé mould and leave in the freezer for about 4 hours, or until the soufflé is lightly frozen. If you are making it beforehand, and it is frozen hard, take it out of the freezer about 1 hour before you want to eat it and leave it in the refrigerator.

Remove the paper collar before serving.

Pots de Crème à l'Orange   Serves 8

2 medium oranges	*2 medium oranges*
2 tbs Grand Marnier	*2–3 tbs Grand Marnier*
4 oz (100 g) caster sugar	*scant ¾ cup superfine sugar*
6 egg-yolks	*6 egg-yolks*
generous 1 pt (650 ml) milk	*generous 2½ cups milk*

Peel the oranges very thinly and cut the zest into very small squares. Blanch for about a minute, drain and refresh, and soak in the Grand Marnier.

Beat the sugar and egg-yolks to a good froth. Bring the milk to the boil and allow to cool slightly before stirring into the mixture. Add the orange zest and the Grand Marnier in which it has been soaking. Pour into small *pots de crème* or ramekins, place the pots in a *bain-marie* and poach in a low oven (275°F, 140°C, gas mark 1) until set (1–1¼ hours). Allow to cool, and put in the refrigerator for at least 2 hours.

With a sharp, pointed knife, remove the skin from the oranges, cutting down to the flesh so that none of the pith remains. Carefully remove each segment of orange by cutting down to the core quite close to the membrane. Use the segments to decorate the creams.

Crème chantilly, or simply some double cream, is not an essential accompaniment to this dish, but is a delicious addition.

Soufflé Glacé aux Noisettes
(Iced Hazelnut Soufflé)

4 eggs	*4 eggs*
3½ oz (90 g) caster sugar	*generous ½ cup superfine sugar*
3 oz (75 g) hazelnut praline (see p27)	*¾ cup hazelnut praline (see p27)*
⅔ pt (350 ml) double cream	*1½ cups whipping cream*
icing sugar	*confectioners' sugar*

Prepare a 1½ pt (1 l, *3½ cup*) soufflé mould by tying round it a collar of greaseproof paper to come about 3″ (7 cm) above the rim. Secure tightly with string or Scotch tape

Beat the egg-yolks and the caster (*superfine*) sugar in a bowl over gently simmering water until they become thick and frothy. Remove from the heat and beat vigorously until cold. Stir in most of the praline, keeping back a little for decoration. In separate basins, beat the egg-whites until they stand in peaks and lightly beat the cream. Mix the egg-whites gently into the praline mixture and gradually fold in the cream. Pour into the mould and freeze for 3 or 4 hours or until just frozen. Before serving, remove the paper collar and sprinkle the top with the rest of the praline mixed with an equal quantity of icing (*confectioners'*) sugar.

If you make the soufflé in advance, so that it is completely frozen, take it out of the freezer about 1 hour before you will be eating it and leave in the refrigerator.

Vacherin à l'Abricot
(Apricot Vacherin)

Serves 8

2 lb (1 kg) fresh apricots	*2 lb fresh apricots*
7 oz (200 g) granulated sugar	*generous 1 cup granulated sugar*
1 pt (½ l) double cream	*2½ cups whipping cream*
6 egg-whites	*6 egg-whites*
12 oz (350 g) caster sugar	*1¾ cups superfine sugar*

The apricots should be cooked on two successive days so that they absorb the syrup: the result will be almost like glacé fruit. Prepare the syrup with the granulated sugar and ½ pt (300 ml, *1¼ cups*) water, boiling together until it just starts to thicken. Cut the apricots in half and remove the stones. Poach gently in the syrup for 10–12 minutes and leave to cool in the syrup. Repeat the next day. Blend and sieve the fruit, and when quite cold mix with half the cream, lightly whipped. Put in the freezer but do not allow to get too hard.

To make the meringue, line three baking trays with foil (*or typing paper*), and mark a 9″ (23 cm) circle on each. Oil lightly. Beat the egg-whites until stiff and standing in peaks. Whisk in half the sugar, whisk again for 2 minutes, then, using a metal spoon, fold in the remaining sugar. Spoon equal amounts of meringue on to each baking tray and spread evenly over the circle with a palette knife. Cook in a very low oven (225°F, 110°C, gas mark ¼) for about 4 hours or until dry. You may need to turn the oven down after the first hour or so, if the meringues are starting to brown.

When you are ready to serve, put one of the meringue rings on a serving dish and spread over it half the apricot filling. Repeat with another ring and the rest of the filling. Put the third ring on top and cover with the remainder of the cream, lightly whipped. Serve at once.

This dessert can also be made with dried apricots (though they wouldn't do so at Saran). In this case you will need 8 oz (225 g, *½ lb*) fruit. Soak for 2–3 hours, until soft, then cook in a syrup composed of 8 oz (225 g, *1½ cups*) sugar and 1 pt (½ l, *2½ cups*) water.

Fresh pineapple is delicious as a fruit base for *vacherin*, but it needs much longer cooking. Cut a large pineapple into small cubes and simmer uncovered in the syrup for a total of 3 hours – 1½ hours each day. Watch carefully towards the end of the second cooking period to see that it is not becoming glutinous. If so, remove from the heat at once. Do not purée the fruit.

Another variation is to substitute vanilla ice for fruit on the bottom layer. Make some *Crème Anglaise* (the quantity given on p22) and freeze. When it is fairly firm spread it over one of the meringue layers and return to the freezer. The ice will be soft enough to serve straight from the freezer.

This dish looks superb if small meringues are arranged all round the sides.

Nougatine Glacée (Praline Ice Cream)

Serves 10

4 egg-whites	*4 egg-whites*
10 oz (275 g) caster sugar	*scant 1½ cups superfine sugar*
8 oz (225 g) almond and hazelnut praline (see p27)	*2 cups almond and hazelnut praline (see p27)*
4 oz (100 g) glacé fruit	*¼ lb glacé fruit*
5 tbs (100 ml) fruit liqueur (mandarine, orange, strawberry or raspberry, according to the flavour of the glacé fruit)	*6 tbs fruit liqueur (mandarine, orange, strawberry or raspberry, according to the flavour of the glacé fruit)*
1 pt (½ l) double cream	*2½ cups whipping cream*
a little jam, fresh fruit or tinned apricots for garnish	*a little jam, fresh fruit or canned apricots for garnish*

First make an Italian meringue. Heat together 4 tbs water and all the sugar except 2 tablespoons, and boil until a temperature of 238°F (116°C) is reached (soft ball stage). Beat the egg-whites as stiffly as possible, adding the remaining 2 tbs sugar towards the end of the beating. Pour the very hot syrup on to the egg-white in a thin, steady stream, beating hard all the time. Continue to beat until the mixture is cold. (A powerful electric beater is needed for this meringue mixture.)

Gently stir the praline into the meringue, then the chopped glacé fruit, the fruit liqueur and the lightly beaten cream. Put into a bombe mould and leave in the freezer for at least 4 hours.

To serve, unmould and surround with a ring of puréed and sieved fresh fruit mixed with a little water. Tinned (*canned*) apricots can be used if fresh fruit is not available, or jam.

Serve straight from the freezer.

Gâteau 'Marronnier' (Cake)   *Serves 8*
(Chestnut Pudding)

Sponge:	*Sponge:*
6 eggs	*6 eggs*
5 oz (150 g) sugar	*¾ cup sugar*
1 teasp vanilla sugar	*1 teasp vanilla sugar*
5 oz (150 g) self-raising flour	*1¼ cups self-rising flour*
Syrup:	*Syrup:*
5 oz (125 g) sugar	*¾ cup sugar*
1–3 tbs rum	*1–3 tbs rum*
Filling:	*Filling:*
3 oz (75 g) butter	*scant ½ cup (¾ stick) butter*
8 oz tin (225 g) sweetened	*½ lb sweetened chestnut purée*
chestnut purée	*¼ lb marrons glacés*
4 oz (100 g) *marrons glacés*	*1 tbs rum*
1 tbs rum	
Garnish:	*Garnish:*
½ pt (300 ml) *crème chantilly*	*1¼ cups crème chantilly (see*
(see p23)	*p23)*
marrons glacés	*marrons glacés*

Sponge: Make this the day before you need it. Beat the egg-yolks to a pale mousse with most of the sugar and the vanilla sugar. Gently incorporate the sifted flour. Whip the egg-whites stiffly, stir into them the remaining sugar and fold into the mixture. Cook in a greased and lined 8″ (20 cm) cake tin in a moderate oven (350°F, 180°C, gas mark 4) for about 35 minutes, or until the sponge is golden and firm in the centre. Turn out of the tin and cool on a rack.

Syrup: Dissolve the sugar in ¼ pt (150 ml, *generous ½ cup*) water and boil until it thickens a little. Add the rum – how much will depend on whether you prefer the flavour to be very mild or rather stronger. Cool.

Filling: Cream the butter and beat in the chestnut purée, the cut-up *marrons glacés* and the rum to make a very light creamy filling.

To assemble: Cut the cake across in three equal slices and lay the bottom slice on a serving dish. Soak it with a third of the syrup. Cover with one-quarter of the filling. Repeat with the other slices, covering the cake all over with the remaining half of the filling. Leave it for at least one hour in a cool place. When you are ready to serve it, completely cover with the *crème chantilly* and decorate with *marrons glacés*.

Tarte aux Raisins
(Grape Tart)

Serves 4

In the Champagne district *Tarte aux Raisins* is the traditional complement to *Potée Champenoise* at the time of the vintage. The tart is usually made in a simpler way than it is in the recipe below – and perhaps is all the more delicious for that – without the addition of the almond base or the meringue topping. In the Champagne region the grapes used are either Pinot Noir (red) or Chardonnay (white). They are packed very tightly in the pastry shell, as they shrink during the cooking, and are sprinkled generously with sugar before the tart is put into the oven.

1 lb (450 g) muscats, or any good white or red grapes	*1 lb muscats, or any good red or white grapes*
6 oz (175 g) shortcrust pastry	*6 oz shortcrust pastry*
3 tbs cognac	*4 tbs cognac*
2 oz (50 g) unsalted butter	*4 tbs (½ stick) unsalted butter*
3½ oz (90 g) caster sugar	*generous ½ cup superfine sugar*
2½ oz (60 g) ground almonds	*1 cup ground almonds*
1 whole egg and 1 egg-white	*1 whole egg and 1 egg-white*

De-pip (*seed*) the grapes, and leave them to marinate in the cognac.

Line an 8″ (20 cm) flan tin (*pie pan*) with the pastry. Prick the bottom with a fork and bake blind for 15 minutes in a fairly hot oven (400°F, 200°C, gas mark 6). Meanwhile, work together the softened butter and a generous half of the sugar so as to obtain a frothy mixture. Add the ground almonds and the egg-yolk. Fill the pastry case with this mixture and return to the oven for a further 10 minutes at the same temperature. Leave to cool.

Arrange the grapes on the tart. Whisk the 2 egg-whites until stiff and spread over the grapes. Sprinkle with the remaining caster (*superfine*) sugar and put in a hot oven till golden. Serve at once.

Gâteau au Fromage Blanc (Cake)

Serves 8

(Cheese Tart)

Sponge cake:

3 eggs
3½ oz (90 g) caster sugar
1 teasp vanilla sugar
3 oz (75 g) self-raising flour

Syrup:

7 oz (200 g) sugar
2–3 tbs kirsch

Filling:

½ pt (300 ml) *crème chantilly*
   (see p23)
2 oz (50 g) caster sugar
3 oz (75 g) cream cheese
6 oz (175 g) raspberry jam

Garnish:

40 cherries *or* 8 oz (225 g)
   strawberries or raspberries
1–2 tbs raspberry jelly

Sponge cake:

3 eggs
generous ½ cup superfine sugar
1 teasp vanilla sugar
¾ cup self-rising flour

Syrup:

generous 1 cup sugar
3–4 tbs kirsch

Filling:

1¼ cups crème chantilly (see p23)
⅓ cup superfine sugar
scant ½ cup cream cheese
6 oz raspberry jam

Garnish:

40 cherries or ½ pint strawberries
   or raspberries
1–2 tbs raspberry jelly

Prepare the sponge cake the day before. Separate the eggs and beat together the yolks, two-thirds of the caster (*superfine*) sugar and the vanilla sugar until light and frothy. Sift the flour and fold carefully into the mixture. Beat the egg-whites until very stiff, and whisk into them the remaining caster sugar. Fold into the mixture. Turn into a greased cake tin, or into two sandwich tins (*tart pans*), and cook in a medium oven (350F, 180C, gas mark 4) for 30 minutes. Turn on to a wire tray.

Next day, cut the sponge into two unless you have made it in two sandwich tins.

Syrup: Boil ¼ pt (150 ml, *generous ½ cup*) water with the sugar until it just starts to thicken, add the kirsch and leave to cool.

Filling: Beat well together the caster (*superfine*) sugar and the cream cheese, and fold in the *crème chantilly*.

154

To assemble: With the handle of a spoon or a pastry brush, force the syrup into the sponge cake. On the first slice spread first the raspberry jam and then a layer of the cream cheese mixture – it should be about 1″ (2 cm) thick. Put the second layer of sponge on top and cover all over with the rest of the cream cheese mixture.

Refrigerate for about 3 hours. To decorate, roll the chosen fruit in the melted raspberry jelly and arrange on top of the cake – but do this at the last possible moment so that the juice does not run out of the fruit. Put back in the refrigerator until ready to serve.

Fraises Opéra — *Serves 6*

1 lb (450 g) strawberries	*1 pint strawberries*
Crème Caramel:	*Crème Caramel:*
1 pt ($\frac{1}{2}$ l) milk	*2$\frac{1}{2}$ cups milk*
vanilla pod	*vanilla bean*
4 eggs	*3 eggs*
6 oz (150 g) caster sugar	*1 cup superfine sugar*
Garnish:	*Garnish:*
4 oz (100 g) small meringues	*$\frac{1}{4}$ lb small meringues*
$\frac{1}{2}$ pt (300 ml) *crème chantilly* (see p23)	*1$\frac{1}{4}$ cups crème chantilly (see p23)*

Crème Caramel: Bring the milk to the boil with the vanilla pod (*bean*). Beat together the eggs and all but 4 tbs of the sugar. Remove the vanilla pod and pour the milk over the eggs, stirring well as you do so. Leave for a few minutes and skim off the foam. Make a caramel with the remaining sugar and line the bottom of a savarin mould with this. Pour in the custard and bake in a *bain-marie* in a coolish oven (325F, 160C, gas mark 3) for about 1 hour, until the custard has set. When it is cold, leave it in the refrigerator for an hour or so.

To serve, unmould the *crème caramel* on to a large round dish and arrange the meringues and the *crème chantilly* in the middle and over the top. Toss the strawberries in a little sugar and arrange them round the outside.

Bananes en Papillotes

For each person:

1 banana	*1 banana*
1 small tbs apricot jam	*1 tbs apricot jam*
a tiny bit of vanilla pod	*a tiny bit of vanilla bean*
nut of butter	*pat of butter*
1–1½ tbs rum	*1–1½ tbs rum*

Cut out a rectangle of aluminium foil about 7" (17 cm) × 10" (25 cm). In this put the banana, the apricot jam, vanilla pod (*bean*), rum and butter. Fold up carefully so that none of the contents can escape, and bake in a hot oven (425°F, 220°C, gas mark 7) for 15–20 minutes.

The bananas should be served in their *papillotes* so that everyone can open his own – a sticky business, so finger-bowls are necessary. But this is a delicious dessert, and well worth buttery fingers.

INDEX

Fish Substitutes P. 58 + 59
Wine Substitutes P. 19

1st Course
Roquefort Soufflé in crepes P. 40
    mushroom ramekins   42
* Délice du Prieur) 43
    (onion tamato mushrooms + chese
        on croutons)
    Melon with Ratafia or Panache 45
        [Soups]
Leek + Potato soup P. 49
Cauliflower + Leek   50
    Tomato Soup (onion chickenbroth cream 51
* Celeriac Soup   52
* Sole - mushroom soup   56
        [Fish]

Salmon with Shallot + mushroom Sauce 60
Sole with mushrooms + tomatos   63
* Sole with Orange sauce
    surrounded by spinach   65
** Sole with Onion in baked
    tomato halves   — 66
** Sea Bass with fennel   P. 72
    Garnish pieces of cucumber   73
        stuffed with tuna + mayonnase
* Turbot layered with mousseline +
        spinach   — 74
    Fish with Beurre Blanc sauce
        surrounded by sautéed cucumber 78
Ham P. 103 [meats]   olives
Beef roulades with sausage   89
* Sweetbreads + Leeks with Sauce P. 93
    Leg of lamb with tarragon   97
    Stuffed shoulder of lamb   — 98
        gr. pork, spinach etc
    Roast pork loin - rice + ham timbales 100

Poultry + Game

* Chicken with Artichokes + small sausages + bacon P. 1
- Chicken with champagne + cognac P. 1
* Roast chicken with herb mixt. under the skin 116
  Poached chicken — Chive sauce 11
* Duck with bitter orange sauce 11
  Duck with green peppercorns 120
* Chartreuse of Cabbage, Sausage, Pretty 1
* Rabbit with mustard P. 129

Veg. + Misc.

Cucumber, olives — 78
Cucumbers stuffed with tuna-mayonnaise
* Julienne potato pancake 117
  Mousse of Pears + Spinach 122
  Onions + sherry 122
  Rice + ham Timbales — 100

Desserts

Profiteroles, Fruit + Sabayon 140
Champagne Sabayon sauce 138
Marquis Alice (Bavarian - Praline) 141
Orange ice cream 143
X X Crème favorite — 144
  Chunks of meringue frozen
  with whipped cream
  Champagne Sorbet — 145
* Iced Coffee soufflé — 146
  Cake - cream cheese filling 154
  Bananas en papillote — 156 148
  Orange Pots de Crème — 149
* Hazelnut Iced soufflé — 149
X X X Sponge cake - Chestnut butter cream 152
  Soak raisins in tea 142
X X Grape Tart 153